A

SEASON

OF

GRACE

*Embracing
God's Gifts in the
Autumn of Our Lives*

A SEASON OF GRACE

Embracing God's Gifts in the Autumn of Our Lives

CAROLYN BASSETT

Published by The Word Among Us Press
7115 Guilford Road
Frederick, Maryland 21704
www.wau.org

21 20 19 18 17   2 3 4 5 6

ISBN: 978-1-59325-316-5
eISBN: 978-1-59325-498-8

Cover design by Faceout
Author photo courtesy of Tom Bassett

Made and printed in the United States of America

Library of Congress Control Number: 2017952038

To Frank, my loving and faithful husband of fifty-three years. It has been my deep joy to share our life together in Christ over these many years with family, friends and those we meet along the way.

Contents

Introduction

In 1975 our pastor at St. Anthony's Parish in Kailua, Hawaii, Fr. Joseph Ferrario, hosted a get-together at his rectory for four couples. We had just finished a lovely meal when Fr. Joe asked us to come into the living room. As we settled in, he said, "I consider myself something like a talent scout for God. I would like to go around the room and share with each of you a gift I believe God has given you and how you might be able to develop it further to help build up the Church."

When my turn came, I was totally surprised by what Fr. Joe said. He thought I had an ability to listen well to others, to affirm them, and to encourage them. He also thought I would be effective with older and infirm people. He suggested that I take some courses with the Diocese of Honolulu on caring for the elderly and dying. He also wanted me to consider joining the chaplaincy at the local hospital.

I looked at my husband, Frank, with disbelief. Me, work with the elderly and the dying in a hospital? Fr. Joe must have been mistaken. I was scared to death to set foot in a hospital. Besides, I was a busy woman, a wife and a mother of two children who was also working part-time. I was fully involved in supporting our son and daughter at school and in sports. Frank and I were also active in our parish and members of a large prayer group at St. Anthony's.

However, after praying for a time, I came to believe that God was asking me to trust him in this work. He wanted me to embrace the new gifts he would give me to do this service. And I not only needed to embrace the new gifts; I also needed to grow more in my trust in him.

It took me almost a year to get over my fear of hospitals. But the more training I received, the more confidence I had that the Holy Spirit could work within me for each person whom I would encounter. This ministry involved me not only with the patients but often with their families as well.

Many of these dear people gave me glimpses into the aging process and the blessing that those who are older could be to others within the family circle and to friends. Some men and women of faith profoundly affected their loved ones as they faced various health issues and other trials and struggled to learn what God wanted to accomplish within them during those times. Others, having more time to live here on earth, were inspired to love with new purpose. As the psalmist wrote, they would "flourish like a palm tree, / . . . still bear fruit in old age," and "stay fresh and green" (Psalm 92:12, 14, NIV). Still others showed me great humility and love in being able to forgive deep hurts of the past. I was also inspired by the many expressions of gratitude for each new day that I heard from many in this season of grace.

Now, four decades later, I have welcomed my aging years with all they entail, even though many days I still feel young at heart. I am writing about what you and I could face as we age and what I have witnessed in the lives of others that has been an encouragement to me.

If you have already reached an esteemed old age, you will probably relate to many of the people on the following pages. My hope is that what you find in common with them will lift your heart, make you smile, and help you to embrace even more from our loving, generous God. This is a season of your life that can bear much fruit for God's kingdom. I hope that you will be inspired to share your stories with others, the young as well as the old, from your personal history, your family history, and your faith journey.

This book is also for those of you who enjoy stories—true stories about real people who are seeking deeper meaning in life as they age, who embrace each day and treasure it for the gift it is, and who grow in love of God and others in the midst of their own limitations and suffering. These stories give you a snapshot of the loving Christ, the merciful and forgiving Christ, the wounded Christ, the suffering Christ, the dying Christ, and the Christ who has risen and is calling you by name. These vignettes also address the misconceptions of aging and point out the advantages and joys of living well as we continue to age. They can help lift your mind and heart to have hope in a real, vibrant, living Christ who is involved in your world and the world at large.

Use this book in your prayer time, as a daily pick-me-up, and as a guide to help you think through difficult situations. I hope it will give you some fresh ideas about building friendships and encourage you to help others grow in their faith in Jesus.

But this book isn't only for those who have already reached the autumn of their lives. If you are interested in the aging process and want to learn more about it now—before you become eligible for those senior discounts!—then these reflections might help you embrace the years to come as well as the gifts that God can give you along the way. It can also be a resource for those who want to help their parents as they age and for anyone who enjoys older people and wants to learn how to relate to them better and support them more fully.

I pray that as you read these vignettes, no matter what

age you may be, you will discover the new gifts that God wants you to embrace and be refreshed in the gifts that you already have. Above all, I hope that your love for Jesus will grow deeper as you see him acting in the lives of those you encounter in the following pages. I welcome you to join me and those I have written about to get a glimpse of what a season of grace could mean for you or for a loved one in the future.

Carolyn Bassett

Aging with a Purpose

Are you aging with a purpose, or are you just aging despite every attempt to resist yet another birthday? Perhaps you view aging as a dreaded process: more aches, more pains, more disease and limitations encroaching on that body of yours. Even if you are relatively healthy, if you lack a heartfelt purpose for each day, you could find depression, apathy, or self-centeredness setting in.

We may be quite aware of God's love for us and may have made a decision to spend time with him daily in prayer. Yet it can still be difficult at times to endure the painful process of change within ourselves. It helps to know that God is revealing his love for us and desires our relationship with him to continue to grow. He will give us the desire to find even deeper meaning in life. Most often his plan for us is found within our family, among our friends, or within our parish.

No matter where we find ourselves, we can learn much from those who have gone before us, including the saints. St. Thérèse of Lisieux, who never left her convent, is known as the patroness of missionaries because of her faithfulness to intercessory prayer. Her calling came from her relationship with Jesus over time, and part of her journey was learning to accept the many limitations she faced because of her physical weakness and illness. Offering up her sufferings through prayer was part of God's plan for her and the way in which she built up the body of Christ. She was certain that she pleased Jesus in this way, and that gave her the determination to love him in and through her suffering until she drew her last breath. Her "little way of love" won the hearts of millions around the world, as she gave them hope that they, too, could please God through loving him in the smallest ways and most difficult of circumstances.

Let us consider where we find ourselves in this process of aging and what more the Lord may want to do within and for us.

Father, life is your gift to me, and my life has purpose because of your love for me. I ask that you refine your love and mercy within me. Let me see the importance of being present to others, growing in grace, and being filled with your Spirit—right up to the moment I see you face-to-face. ⌣

He Is Listening

From the beginning of time, God sought out a people with whom he could communicate, share his heart of love, and show what is really important to him. Our Father is pursuing you, inviting you to communicate with him and to share with him your joys and sorrows, your fears and anxieties, your frustrations, your concerns about the future, as well as the hopes you hold dear to your heart. He is listening, hoping to be invited into your world as you go about your day. He is listening for you to call his name.

I have two young friends who have shown me much about our Father's tenderness, about his ability to lean forward into our lives and listen carefully to what we are saying and to what we want to say but just cannot. My young friends are named Emily and Rebecca. They both were born with Down syndrome. They both come from loving, caring families. They both treasure friendships and look forward to spending time with people. They both love going to church and receiving the sacraments.

As I have spent time with Emily and Rebecca, I have realized that they have much to share. So I have tried to capture what is on their hearts. I need to listen carefully, not only to the words they speak, but also to the emotions they show on their faces and the way they use their hands to express themselves. These beautiful young ladies will never fully know how much of our Father's heart I have seen in them and the joy I feel being with them. To me they are part of our Father's presence in our complicated world today.

Dear friend, you are deeply loved by our Father, much more than you will ever realize. He longs to communicate with you, listen to you, and share his heart with you. Will you make some extra time today to be still and let him love you as only he can?

Father, you created me to be in a loving relationship with you. Often I don't understand what you are saying to me because I don't take the time to be still and listen. Teach me, Lord, to wait upon you. ___

Free at Last

As we journey through life, we want to enjoy our last years and experience increasing peace. Most of the time, finding that peace of mind and heart takes some work on our part, including the willingness and the humility to forgive.

In my years of working in hospital chaplaincy, I encountered people who had lived good Christian lives but who, in approaching death, realized that there was a relationship or two that had yet to be reconciled. In some cases, the relationships that were most meaningful to them had caused them the deepest pain.

Brenda was dying of lung cancer, and she was not at peace. A key relationship in her life haunted her. Brenda's mother had died when she was quite young, and her stepmother had not been kind to her. Time and again, Brenda would talk about the many times this woman had ignored her needs, screamed at her, and shut her out of the house.

Growing up, Brenda had two saving graces. She played the organ at Mass in two small churches, which brought her much joy and affirmation. She also had a neighbor who knew her plight and often took her in to show her kindness and a listening ear.

Brenda had tried to forgive her stepmother but could not let go of her deep hurts. Then, toward the end of her life, while in the ICU, she asked me to come to visit her. She wanted to tell me something.

Early that morning, at the end of her bed, Brenda saw Jesus and her kind neighbor, as well as the bishop who had praised her for playing the organ all those years. She was so moved by their love for her that she wanted to forgive her stepmother. In tears we prayed together, and she was able to express her complete forgiveness. She had her confession heard and was ready to go home. She was free at last! She died in peace, surrounded by her family.

We can learn a lot from Brenda. It is never too late to humble ourselves and forgive, even if the hurt is very deep. God our Father knows our weakness and will help us. He wants to rid us of any impediment to our journey into eternity.

Jesus, you promised you would go before us, prepare a place for us, and come to take us home. Help me put all my trust in you. ⌒

Hospitality

Are you the kind of person who enjoys being surprised? When we were younger, we may have loved an unexpected knock on the door from a friend who wanted to visit or go for a walk or just chat for a while. The flexibility of youth is a beautiful thing.

However, research shows that as we age, we can become more rigid and set in our ways. We may be unable to adjust easily to new circumstances, or we may be less open to new ideas or to someone "intruding" on our schedule for the day. This may make us less receptive to showing and practicing hospitality.

Yet we don't have to become another research statistic! We have the Holy Spirit, who brings us new life day by day, refreshes and inspires us, and fills us with the love of Christ. Love is open to the present moment and inspires us to be generous.

We have a dear friend who will sometimes call and say, "I know this is last minute, but could you all join us for dinner tonight?" Even though she has done this a number of times, I am always surprised when she calls. My spirits are lifted, and I know we will be blessed to share a meal with her family.

God created us to relate to one another, to share life together, to share meals together, and to just spend time together. The body of Christ builds itself up in love. My friend's example of spontaneity, generosity, and faithfulness inspires me. I often come home wanting to do more and believing I can do more for others.

There are many examples of hospitality in Scripture. One of my favorites is the story of Peter's mother-in-law (Mark 1:29-31). There she was, in bed and suffering with a high fever, when Jesus entered the home. Moved by compassion, Jesus surprised her by standing over her and rebuking the fever. Immediately she got up and began to serve Jesus and his disciples. She must have felt so loved by him. With her newfound energy, she did what came naturally to her: she served them all!

You, too, are embraced by God's love, and that love can inspire your heart and mind to be more spontaneous and responsive. Our Father will use whatever you offer him to bless and build up others.

Father, each day is new and fresh with your Holy Spirit residing within me. Bless my mind and heart with an awareness of your great love for me. Help me to be more open to others and to share your love at any given moment.

Loneliness

Did you know that the proportion of Americans who live alone has grown steadily since the 1920s? With families more spread out geographically, fewer aging adults live near or with adult children. And many older people choose to live alone because they value their independence.

For years it was common to see the three-generation family living together. Parents and their children benefited from the presence of older family members. The older generation was able to share wisdom and the history of the family. The elders also shared their love and faith with their grandchildren. The grandparents were needed in small but significant ways. This added to their sense of dignity and contentment, as they realized that God had a continuing purpose for their lives as they aged.

The changes in our culture make it more likely today that older adults experience loneliness and isolation. While anyone can feel lonely from time to time, those who are in their later years are particularly at risk. Isolation can lead to depression and a lack of vision about the deeper meaning of life in the senior years.

What about those of us who cannot live with family for a variety of reasons yet would like to be more connected to them, as well as to friends and the wider community? We have many choices to consider.

After becoming a widow, Rosie chose to move closer to her family. Now she helps out with carpooling and can more easily attend special events that her grandchildren are involved in, as well as invite them over for meals.

Another woman, Kathleen, became friendly with her younger neighbors and their children. This led to her offering to help the children with their homework assignments, even tutoring them in math.

Most churches have outreaches for seniors that can include Bible study and social events. These gatherings are wonderful ways to meet new friends as well as to grow in our relationship with Christ.

As you age, what can you do to make sure you do not isolate yourself from others? What changes can you make to communicate more with family and friends? How can you use your experience of loneliness to bless someone else?

Father, I am part of your family, yet sometimes I feel forgotten by others. Inspire me today to set aside my sadness and call one person who might be lonely. ⌣

Sharing Our Faith

Have you ever struggled with sharing your faith with others? If so, you are not alone. It is difficult at times to talk about what our Lord has done for us, especially with family members.

One summer, while on vacation with our family, I was praying for our grandchildren and was surprised by an inner prompting to share a story about my faith journey with one of them. Over the next few days, I looked for an opportunity to have a one-on-one conversation, but the house was always full of activity. Finally, the moment I was anticipating arrived. I walked through the dining area and saw Tom sitting alone, working on the computer. With some fear and trepidation in my heart, I seized the moment! As I sat down, it came to me in an instant what I was going to share.

I told the story of how God had intervened in my life many years earlier, through people who had prayed with me at a parish prayer meeting. It had been a very difficult time for our family. My husband, Frank, was serving at the US embassy in Cambodia; our son, Mark, was thirteen, and our daughter, Tina, only five. When I was prayed with, I experienced the love of a heavenly

Father reaching out to me, impressing upon my heart the need to trust him one day at a time. This experience radically transformed my relationship with the Lord.

What I didn't know at the time was that Frank's life would soon be in grave danger. Within a few months, the embassy staff was airlifted out of Phnom Penh, only twelve hours before the capital fell to Communist insurgents. Looking back, I realized that God in his great mercy had reached out to me and to my family at a crucial moment and drawn us to himself. My relationship with him continues to grow to this day.

As my conversation with Tom progressed, I realized that the fear I had felt was being transformed into great love. It was as though the Lord had been waiting for me to act in faith, trusting in him. This grandchild had never heard me speak so openly about this important time in my life. He thanked me for caring enough to share my story.

Father, I want to be freer to share the good news about your unconditional love. Help me to trust in you more fully. ___

An Ordinary Day

The year was 1948, and I was looking forward to visiting the home of my great-aunts Rachel and Lizzie. My Aunt Helen and Grandmother Matilda would often take me when they dropped by in the summer. Aunt Rachel and Aunt Lizzie, registered nurses who did home care, often had stories to tell of how God had come to the aid of someone they were caring for. I loved to hear these older women tell their stories! We would sit in the parlor sipping tea, and as they talked, the whole room would seem to be filled with light.

That day's visit, however, was quite different from the norm. Before I left home, my mother told me that Aunt Rachel had fallen asleep in Christ. I didn't really comprehend what that meant, since I had never had a close family member die.

Upon entering the parlor, everything looked the same, except that Aunt Rachel was lying in a plain, bed-like box with her church dress on and smiling sweetly with her eyes closed. I walked up close to her and stood looking at her with great love, and I suddenly realized that never again would I hear her tell her wonderful stories.

We sat down for our tea, and Aunt Lizzie recalled many memories of her sister. I was comforted that we were in their parlor. Later, when my father came home from work, he joined my mother and me to again visit their home, and our conversation about dear Aunt Rachel continued.

That memory is a precious one, filled with peace and love. The experience set the foundation of how I see death: an ordinary part of life because of our faith in Christ our Lord, a passing from this life into life eternal.

"Do not let your hearts be troubled. Believe in God, believe also in me. In my Father's house there are many dwelling places. . . . And if I go and prepare a place for you, I will come again and will take you to myself, so that where I am, there you may be also" (John 14:1-2, 3). Life is not ended but continued in the fullness of what life is meant to be in Christ.

What thoughts come to mind as you read and pray about this Scripture passage?

Jesus, open my heart and eyes to the beauty of passing from one life to another in Christ. Help me be an encouragement to others who may be suffering or even close to death.

It's Never Too Late

We all have natural gifts and talents. Some we use early in our lives, while others may lie dormant for years and then blossom later in life.

Julia Child's personal interest in food started in 1948, when she moved with her husband to Paris and tasted French cuisine for the first time. She began hosting *The French Chef* in 1963, at the age of fifty. Her simplified approach to French cooking made her a television favorite for many decades.

Sometimes it takes another person to encourage us to use a particular gift or talent that we don't even know we have. Laura Ingalls Wilder's *Little House on the Prairie* books have captured the imagination of generations of American schoolchildren, but they were written when the author was in her golden years. It was through the urging of Wilder's daughter that she took up writing.

Whichever way our gifts may be awakened, God will use them to build up his body. Our gifts and talents are meant to be shared and consequently to grow.

Anne was in her forties when she was prayed with for a greater outpouring of Jesus' love in her life. The experience of giving her life to Christ was transformative, and she wanted to share it. She discovered that she could write poetry to express God's love for others. Many found comfort, hope, and joy through her poems.

At the age of sixty-five, Anne wrote her first book, and then a second one when she was seventy-five. Even though her eyesight has now grown quite dim, at the age of eighty-five, Anne still writes poems for Christmas, Easter, Hanukkah, and Passover. With the help of others, she mails them to her many friends.

It is important that we remain open to the inspirations of the Holy Spirit, the giver of all gifts. We may think it is too late to receive or use a particular gift; however, God's timing is always perfect. We are never too old to use our gifts to build up our brothers and sisters, and God is always honored in the process!

Holy Spirit, help me to share your gifts so that I may be your presence in my world today.

Friends of All Ages

As we age, it is important that we continue to invest time and energy to keep up with our friends. Perhaps you enjoy getting together with friends for a book club or Bible study, an exercise class, or simply a walk in the park. Maybe you enjoy sharing a cup of tea. Spending time with friends is good for the soul. It's also just plain fun.

It is especially good to have friends of all ages. One friend who is fifteen years younger than I will call and say, "Do you have time for me to stop by today or tomorrow? We could take a walk or just sit and talk for a while." Sometimes we take a trip to the store or have a bite for lunch. Our time together is always a mixture of conversation and laughter and at times even tears. She energizes and encourages me with her more youthful, faith-filled perspective on life as well as her faithfulness as a friend.

Another friend is ten years older than I. She has early-onset dementia, yet because of her deep faith, she has a hopeful perspective. She frequently says, "I have a tendency to talk too much; why don't you share first what is going on in your life?" I learn much from her. I admire her humility in accepting her illness and joining it to the sufferings of Christ. I also find her transparency refreshing.

I have a few friends who are widows, and I observe them grieving without losing hope. I am inspired by their courage and determination to continue to be involved in life, giving to their families and others.

Friendship can lift our hearts and minds to see our cups half full rather than half empty. Friends can also give us a new perspective on our struggles. How many times have you had a conversation with a close friend about something that was troubling you and later had a new insight? Or maybe your heart was more at peace. Our friends can be God's special gifts in this season of our lives. "These God-chosen lives all around—what splendid friends they make!" (Psalm 16:3, *The Message*).

Father, my friends are an expression of your love for me, your generous gifts during this season of my life. Thank you! ⌢

Children and Loss

Feelings of deep sadness are no respecter of age; even children grieve the loss of someone dear to them. How children work through grief is different from how most adults go through it. Have you ever helped a child work through sadness due to the loss of someone dear to him or her?

Our role as grandparent or friend of a young person can be one of support during difficult times. We can help bring comfort to children if we know them well.

While visiting our family one Thanksgiving, I was reading a book with our six-year-old granddaughter when she started to cry. I held her in my arms as she told me that she was really sad that Uncle Tommy had died, and she would miss him at Christmas when everyone got together for the family party. Mae likes to draw, so I asked her if she would like to draw a picture of Uncle Tommy.

We took a trip to the craft store, and Mae chose a special binder and some pretty colored pens. When she had finished her drawing, she came to me beaming, holding out her picture. To my surprise, she had drawn a beautiful angel. She proudly announced that this was

Uncle Tommy's guardian angel, who had taken him to heaven. I had tears in my eyes, moved by the faith of this innocent child. She went on to write a letter to her uncle about how she missed him but was happy he was in heaven.

This was just the beginning. Mae decided to draw a guardian angel for each member of the family. She added them to the binder and called it *The God Book*.

Years later this child, at the age of fourteen, sent me a text that said, "God's Not Dead," after seeing the movie with the same title. This time it was she who was reaching out to me in a loving gesture that inspired me to have greater trust in our God.

It is important for us to remember that as grandparents, we are building special memories with our grandchildren that they will carry with them through life. These memories, built on God's love, can provide a way for their faith as well as ours to be strengthened.

Father, thank you for the gift of young people. Help me respond lovingly and wisely when they struggle with life's challenges. ⎯

Movements within the Heart

Remember the Gospel story of the two disciples traveling on the road to Emmaus (Luke 24:13-25)? Walking along and talking solemnly about what had just transpired in Jerusalem, they were suddenly joined by a stranger who became part of the conversation. But this was no ordinary conversation. The hearts of these two disciples were captivated; they were totally drawn to the stranger's words and his presence. So they asked him to stay for supper, and in the breaking of the bread, they recognized that this fellow traveler was Jesus!

The lives of these two disciples were changed by that encounter, and so can your life and mine be any time we encounter Jesus in prayer. A regular time each day dedicated to personal prayer can become the springboard for an intimate relationship with our Father—a conversation of the heart, when we are completely ourselves and at ease with him.

We can spend part of that time of day, perhaps fifteen minutes or half an hour, reading the Scriptures. In this way, we come to know our Father through Jesus and the movements of his heart. For example, seeing Jesus' compassion, as when he raised the widow's son from the dead (Luke 7:11-17), we come to know the Father and can draw closer to his heart. In our Father's heart, we will, like that widow, encounter his compassion and mercy.

But like the disciples on the road to Emmaus, we have to linger with Jesus. It will take time and attention for our relationship and love for our Lord to grow. Meeting with him daily will require a commitment of our hearts. It will mean setting aside time to listen to what he might be saying to us.

Personal prayer is an adventure. Once we give our hearts to the Lord and become focused on him, we become captivated by his love. Then our natural response is to praise and worship him. And the more time we spend in his presence, the more we will want to be with him. Like the disciples on the road to Emmaus, we will say, "Were not our hearts burning within us while he was talking to us?" (Luke 24:32).

Father, your love for me has captivated my heart. Help me get to know you better and be able to recognize you more clearly as you act in my life. ⸺

Responding to Life's Crises

Where were you on September 11, 2001? Nearly all of us can recall the exact moment. The shock of realizing that security in the United States had failed and that thousands of people had been killed within minutes left the entire nation numb.

Even though it may be painful to recall the events of 9/11, there may be some things that we can learn about ourselves by reviewing that day. How did we react when we first heard the news? Did we take a few minutes to turn to the Lord, asking for his guidance, wisdom, and grace before we acted?

Even in the shock of a given moment, the Holy Spirit can empower us in our weakness and bring clarity. The following examples show how the Holy Spirit inspired a few people to go into action after the tragic event.

One older woman I know started cooking as much comfort food as she could. Members of the family she was staying with were returning home from New York that day, after seeing the Twin Towers hit as their airplane landed at JFK Airport.

One grandfather noticed a grandson in his home who sat staring blankly at the TV, stunned that the United

States had been so brutally attacked. The boy needed to talk, to be encouraged. Grandpa was there to listen and to comfort.

Another woman, a nurse, signed up to go and help out in New York. She tended the wounded and interacted with their families.

At least one family gathered that evening to pray the Rosary. Many people went to special church services or attended Mass.

We never know when there will be a crisis or an emergency of some sort. However, we can be confident that the Holy Spirit will bring to mind what can be helpful in the situation. God may give us a new gift to use at that moment or renew a gift within us.

And sometimes the best and only thing we can do in a crisis is to pray for others. Even then we are included in the economy of God's grace, helping by our prayers to bring good out of tragedy.

Father, you promise to never leave me or forsake me. When there is a crisis, remind me to turn to you and rely on your Holy Spirit. In you I place my trust. ⌣

A Season of Transition

As we age, one of the most difficult obstacles to work through is the realization that our world is becoming smaller. We retire, and our lifestyles and routines are altered. Family members and friends pass away. And perhaps the influence we had with others is no longer needed in the same way. We enter into a new season—the autumn of our lives.

The East Coast, where I live, is especially beautiful in the autumn. The leaves turn to brilliant yellows and oranges and deep reds and browns before they fall to the ground and die, leaving room for new life to emerge in the spring. God's creation lets go of the old and welcomes new life.

As each change in our life comes, we can take the time to pray, think, discern, and talk to a trusted friend about what God is saying to us. Which gifts is he offering us, and how can we embrace these gifts? What would we like to do next?

After Dave's death, Kathy experienced deep loss and grief. She and Dave were quite a team; they were known for their generous gift of hospitality. Their table was often filled with people and lively conversation! Now, in the midst of her grief, Kathy's love and support for family and friends continued and were beautiful to observe. A few years later, a new door opened for her: she gathered a group of women to meet regularly to grow in their friendship with Christ and with one another.

Each one of us will have our own personal experiences in the autumn of our lives. We can count on the fact that each day, God's grace is new, helping us to transition and work through difficulties and the adjustments we need to make. He will give us new insights and the grace to live our lives to the full, experiencing new delights one day at a time.

God our Father, I am so very grateful that you have ushered me into this season of my life. I pray that my heart and mind will continue to be open to your love and inspiration. Help me to be a shelter to those in need and to be generous in love to all you send to me. ⁓

A Sacred Space

There are many things vying for our attention today. Without ever leaving our homes, at any time of day, we can get news from around the world, be entertained with the latest reality show or movie, or shop to our heart's delight—all with one click of a mouse or remote.

All the more reason to give some attention to finding or creating a place where we can pray—a space where there are few distractions, where it is easy to be present to the living God. Maybe that will be in a quiet church before Mass starts or at an adoration chapel. When I pray before the Blessed Sacrament, I sense an atmosphere of peace and love that warms my heart, and my conversation with Jesus seems to flow more easily.

A friend who is a trauma therapist has given a great deal of thought, attention, and prayer to how she furnishes her office. The placement of the furniture, the pictures, and the lighting are important. She has set a tone for her clients to enable them to relax and be present. Her office is a place where they can find connection, healing, and hope for the future.

Each of us can create a sacred space in our homes where there are few distractions and where we find it easier to pray. It may be just a corner of a room where we place an icon, a candle, or a crucifix. It could be a whole room dedicated to prayer.

Jesus wants your attention. He wants your friendship with him to deepen. He loves you and will help you understand his love for you more clearly. He invites you to come into his presence daily—to talk with him and to bring him your concerns, your distractions, your hopes, and your dreams. Give yourself permission to be still so that you can be loved deeply by the one person who has made it possible for you to be free and experience life fully.

Jesus, I want to make more room in my heart for you. I want to be more present to you, to be able to have a deeper appreciation for your amazing love and faithfulness. Help me to find a sacred space where I can talk with and listen to you. ——

The Journey of Forgiveness

Have you ever met someone who says he or she has forgiven another person yet repeats the same sad story of hurt, betrayal, abuse, or rejection over and over again? I think we would agree that forgiveness from the heart is not always an easy matter! It takes the grace, mercy, and love of Jesus working within us.

The deeper the hurt, the more grace it may take. In fact, in some cases, forgiveness can be called a journey, with progressive stages of understanding and growth. So let us not lose heart if we feel stuck remembering hurt and rejection from the past.

In his Letter to the Elderly, Pope St. John Paul II wrote, "Dear brothers and sisters, at our age it is natural to revisit the past in order to attempt a sort of assessment. . . . The passage of time helps us to see our experiences in a clearer light."[1] With this encouraging word, let us remember that whatever degree of hurt we have experienced or may still struggle with, God is with us and can help us grow toward a deeper understanding of his mercy and love.

A woman who had suffered verbal and physical abuse from her husband for some years eventually separated from him, and they divorced. For many years, she struggled with truly forgiving him. As she looked back over her life, a very wise person asked her, "What was the harvest the Lord brought out of this very difficult period of your life?"

Later, while the woman was praying about this question, she realized that out of this tragedy she had found the pearl of great price, Jesus Christ! The Lord's presence had changed her life. This new insight gave her more freedom to love, to be loved, and to forgive.

When we forgive another, our hearts can become enlarged, able to hold even more of God's grace and love. Just as the Holy Spirit enlightened this woman, he will enlighten you to help bring more clarity and freedom to your soul.

Jesus, your forgiveness is unlimited. Show me if I am holding on to a past hurt. If I am unable to forgive a person, help me to know whom to talk to about my struggle. Give me hope to know greater freedom in my soul, for I desire to love you and others more and more. ⸺

Heroic Love

As we age, we may suffer with health issues or have physical limitations or handicaps. They can make us feel as if it is more difficult to love and to reach out to others. If such is the case, it is helpful to follow St. Thérèse of Lisieux's "little way." She wrote, "What matters in life is not great deeds but great love." We can find an avenue to love in all circumstances.

A lawyer who had reached the top of his profession served for many years in an important government position and eventually received a special award from the president for his outstanding work. This man said proudly, "I gave 100 percent of my energy to my profession." Later he recalled this statement with regret, as he realized that he had missed many opportunities to show love to his wife and daughters.

When this man was diagnosed with cancer, he thought that perhaps treatment would lead to remission. The cancer only continued to spread, even with aggressive protocols. Yet despite the odds against him, he outlived the statistics the first year after his diagnosis. It was then that a dream began to emerge of how he could show great love to his wife and daughters.

He created a file of everything in their home that needed to be fixed—large items down to smaller ones, like lamps and toilets. He then created a list of new furnishings and window treatments, to update the home and put it in tip-top shape. He spent time getting estimates and choosing contractors. Day and night, he oversaw the work, all while suffering and growing weaker.

Along the way, after years of hurt and disappointment, the man and his wife were reconciled. When the wife told me about the reconciliation, her face was radiant with joy and peace. The doors of God's mercy had opened wide for this family to enjoy relating to one another in new freedom and love. The man later died a peaceful death, surrounded by his family.

Within a given day, you and I make many choices. Let us pray that our choices help promote love, life, and peace.

Jesus, my time with you in prayer unites me more closely to your loving heart and empowers me to love others more effectively. Show me the way to love others even when I am struggling. ——

The Lord's Faithfulness

Let your steadfast love, O LORD, be upon us.
—PSALM 33:22

As we age, we are faced with circumstances that we might not have chosen. So it is good to be reminded of God's presence and love with short Scripture verses like the one above. They remind us of the truth of God's love and provision for us in every season of our lives.

A very good and gifted priest had worked hard for years in the Church and among God's people to help bring them closer to Jesus. He had even served the Church in other countries, helping to establish new parishes while serving the poor. He eventually retired and lived with other priests in a retirement facility. The transition to a slower, more confined lifestyle went well. He said Mass, spent more time in prayer, kept in touch with family and friends, and sometimes had visitors. He knew the value of slowing down and of being alone at times, to be refreshed and renewed by the Lord.

As time went on, however, this priest realized that he was getting fewer phone calls. He was also disappointed by the decreased response to his calls to others.

The growing silence of the answering service became too painful, so he had the service discontinued. Because few really cared or took the time to visit, he felt that he was a forgotten man, and he experienced a deep sense of loneliness.

However, he never felt abandoned by God. He lived these words of the psalmist: "Teach us to number our days, / that we may gain a heart of wisdom" (Psalm 90:12, NIV). His wisdom over the years came from his constant closeness to the Lord. He remained bound by love to God our Father, even when things were difficult. While he missed the encouragement and friendship of some in the body of Christ, he simply forgave those who disappointed him.

Are we bound to God in the same way? Do we know, in the deepest recesses of our hearts, that the Lord will never abandon us, even if everyone else does?

Father, your constant love gives me confidence that you will be with me, no matter what the future holds. Help me to be faithful to those who I know are going through difficult changes in life. ___

Grieving with Hope

Most of us have experienced deep sorrow over the death of someone close to us. It's as if our world has stopped and is closing in on us. We may initially be in a state of shock, which helps protect us from the raw emotions that separation brings. Eventually, however, we need to enter the process of grieving—helped by the hope of the resurrection and by friends who can accompany us along the way.

Jesus knew we would need his wisdom and compassion when facing death. When telling his disciples of his own upcoming death, he said, "A little while, and you will no longer see me, and again a little while, and you will see me. . . . Very truly, I tell you, you will weep and mourn . . . ; you will have pain, but your pain will turn into joy" (John 16:16, 20). Jesus was holding out to the disciples hope of his own resurrection and the promise that they would one day be together again.

Jesus also knew personally what it meant to grieve deeply. We recall his weeping over the death of Lazarus (see John 11). Surrounded by Mary, Martha, and the Jews who were gathered with them, he shows us the importance of sharing our grief with friends.

I belong to a small women's group that meets weekly. One night one of the women suddenly began talking about her mother, who had died several months earlier. She had talked about her mother before, but this was one of those moments when grief broke through her usual composure and expressed itself uninvited. She described what those last few days were like before her mother died, not only for her but for her two sisters as well. A new bonding had taken place between them, she said, and their time together seemed to be their mother's last gift to them. She also expressed the hope they had of being united someday in heaven.

Our conversation continued for some time. She thanked us profusely for staying late, and we all thanked her for being open to share with us.

What has helped you in the grieving process? Have you found it helpful to share your memories of your loved one with a close friend?

Jesus, you call me your friend. Stay with me as I grieve the loss of those dear to me. Teach me to be a faithful friend to others as they grieve. —

Simple Delight

The heavens are telling the glory of God;
and the firmament proclaims his handiwork.
—PSALM 19:1

How do we build a new habit of thanking our Father for his many gifts? We can start by just looking out the window on a given day and delighting in what we see. All of creation is filled with God's beauty, created out of love for us.

My mother's favorite bird was the wren. Wrens are tiny in size but have a loud, clear song. She affectionately called the birds "Jenny Wrens." Mom appreciated their faithfulness: they were always present, whatever the season—spring, summer, fall, or winter. Morning, noon, and early evening, they belted out their song.

My husband, Frank, and I are fortunate to have a family of wrens nesting near our patio. We, too, have learned to appreciate their presence. From morning to dusk, a wren will come to sing her song.

One day when the temperature was well below freezing, "Jenny Wren" appeared at noon. As she was singing, we noticed that her chest was not fully extended and her song was quite faint. She was obviously restricted by the extreme cold air.

We especially appreciated her presence that day and delighted in her song. I had been going through a difficult time, homebound with the flu. Seeing the little wren singing her song, ever so faint in the extreme cold, reminded me that I could choose to be grateful to the Lord that day, even though I was feeling sick and depressed.

God's love constantly surrounds us and can encourage us when we least expect it. We are touched by his imprint of beauty through his creatures and creation. His handiwork can be a source of joy and gratitude for us, whatever the season in which we find ourselves.

Perhaps today we can ask the Lord to show us something in his creation that will delight us, something that reminds us that his love and life are always present.

Father, your creation is full of delightful surprises, beauty, and inspiration. I stand in awe of your presence all around me! —

When the Unexpected Happens

On a snowy day in 1984, my life changed in an instant. I slipped in a church parking lot as I was running and was propelled into the air, falling hard on my side. According to the doctors, the impact was the equivalent of a second-story fall.

As a result of my injuries, I spent the next three months in the hospital in immovable traction. A large steel pin was implanted through my left knee, with a thirty-pound weight at the end. I was stripped of my ability to serve and care for my daughter, husband, and aging mother. At times I felt worthless. I went through periods of anxiety, fear, and doubt, as well as anger. I was forty-four at the time but felt as if I were forty years older.

Gradually, through prayer, God's grace, and the support of my family and friends, I was able to embrace my situation and trust the Lord, even though I had no idea what the future held for me.

On my last day in the hospital, as I was sitting on the edge of my bed, I had a surprise visit. The head nurse of the orthopedic ward and her team of eight nurses came in and lined up against the wall. They had a question for me: "How did you keep from going crazy these past three months?"

At that moment, I had a crystal-clear thought that had been forming in my mind and heart, a gift of new understanding from our Lord. "The most important things in my life never changed—my relationship with God, my family, and my friends. Each morning I have had time to pray and receive the Eucharist, and every day I have had at least one visitor, in person or by telephone."

We all experience trials of various kinds. It will take time and prayer for us to be able to see the good that our Father wants to bring out of our circumstances. What a blessing these times can be if, in the end, we gain new wisdom and understanding of what is truly important in life.

Lord, each day you invite me to come and sit with you, to be in your presence, to listen and respond. Through these times with you, I come to see what really matters in life. Help me to abide more in you as you abide in me. —

Fully Alive

The glory of God is man fully alive.
—ST. IRENAEUS[2]

When we read this quote from the Church Father St. Irenaeus, we might ask ourselves, "Do I really feel *fully* alive?" Our minds might go back to a time when our energy was unlimited, our minds were quick, and we felt fearless and full of adventure. Perhaps we were raising a family or working long hours at a demanding job, or perhaps we could jog long distances pain-free on a regular basis. Life could not have been better!

As we age, we may come to realize that our physical strength has declined. Perhaps our minds seem sluggish at times; it may take a while to recall that name or place. On some days, we might not even have the desire to get out of the house. We could be dealing with a chronic illness that is debilitating or struggling with discouragement or depression.

In his Second Letter to the Corinthians, St. Paul tells us that we are not to lose heart, that while our outer strength is declining, our inner strength is being renewed day by day (see 4:16). What is it that renews us from within?

We are cherished by our Father; he will never leave us or forsake us (see Hebrews 13:5). He calls us his beloved! He wants to spend time with us. He wants to reveal himself to us through Scripture and prayer as well as in the Sacraments of Confession and the Eucharist. His presence refreshes us, gives us peace, and imparts to us a desire to be with him throughout our day.

It doesn't matter what our age is or our state in life or our health condition. We all have that God-given freedom from within to respond to his unconditional love for us. We can say, "Yes, Lord, here I am; I come to do your will" (see Hebrews 10:9).

When we realize that our *yes* to the Lord throughout the day is life giving to ourselves and to others, then our whole being can be transformed and energized. Let us allow ourselves to become more fully alive in Christ!

Father, thank you for reminding me that in you, I am fully alive. Your love for me gives me a peace and blessed assurance that no one else can give. You have given me the opportunity to shine! Give me the grace this day to do your will. ___

Roots

It was a Saturday morning in 1946, and my aunt and grandmother had stopped by our home to pick me up and take me to the cemetery. This was a weekly tradition. I was six, and it was a treat to spend time with my aunt and grandmother all by myself.

Two large buckets full of beautiful cut flowers from their garden rested on the back floor of the car, next to me. I loved the fragrance. But the best part of the ride to and from the cemetery was listening to the conversation of my aunt and grandmother. They laughed easily and treated one another with love and respect.

Once at the cemetery, we would get water from the pumps and fill the permanent vases at the graves of three generations of deceased members of our family. As we placed flowers in the vases, my aunt and grandmother would recall stories of different relatives—faith-filled stories pointing out valuable characteristics of some, along with fun-loving memories. At an early age, I learned a lot about my family heritage and got to know my aunt and grandmother quite well. I also decided that I would like to have that kind of relationship with my mother when we were older.

As I continued to mature into a young woman, there were other characteristics about the two of them that I wanted to develop. They handed down to me a rich tradition of how a Christian woman lives her life and treats others. I never heard my grandmother or aunt say a negative word about anyone. They treated those they knew with dignity and respect, and they were peacemakers within the family.

As I became an adult, I found that it can sometimes be a challenge to say nothing rather than speak ill of someone. To say only the good things people need to hear is a goal to keep striving for and a choice to be made.

Who has inspired you to be more merciful or to live in a particular way? What was it in their lives that caught your attention?

Lord, thank you for the abundant blessings and goodness you have brought into my life through others. Help me to be generous and creative in passing along my faith as well as rich traditions to family members and friends.

Helping Those with Depression

Many of us have probably been depressed at one time or another, and as we age, we can be more vulnerable to depression for a variety of reasons. When we are alert to the symptoms of depression—which include feelings of sadness, periods of inactivity, and difficulty in concentrating or making decisions—we can seek help or help others who are suffering from it.

When I was in my early forties, I was seriously injured in an accident. Even after a three-month stay in the hospital, I spent the better part of the next year in physical therapy. After my release from the hospital, I was depressed. I was dealing with a lot of loss. I could no longer enjoy gardening or jogging with our daughter, who was sixteen at the time. What I didn't know then is that this injury would affect the rest of my life. I would be unable to climb steps normally, limited in the distance I could walk, and needing to do certain exercises daily.

It took me about a year to work through the process of accepting the new normal of my life. I prayed daily to our Father and often used the confessional. In time, as my heart softened and I grew in acceptance of the changes in my life, God showed me how he wanted to use this experience. My mother had suffered a stroke, and I began to understand her occasional frustration. She was feeling the loss of being able to take care of herself and being able to communicate normally.

We can be advocates for those close to us who struggle with depression or loss. As we grow in understanding of the person and what he or she is facing, we can offer our friendship, support, and prayer. We can ask if the doctor knows the whole story and if the person's medications are up to date. In some cases, it might help to accompany someone to a doctor's visit.

God is faithful. As we pray, the Lord will give us what we need to love and encourage our loved ones—friends and family—in their times of need.

Father, your mercy knows no limits. Help me to grow in mercy and be more effective in supporting others close to me. ⌒

Martha and Mary

Now as they went on their way, he entered a certain village, where a woman named Martha welcomed him into her home. She had a sister named Mary, who sat at the Lord's feet and listened to what he was saying. But Martha was distracted by her many tasks; so she came to him and asked, "Lord, do you not care that my sister has left me to do all the work by myself? Tell her then to help me." But the Lord answered her, "Martha, Martha, you are worried and distracted by many things; there is need of only one thing. Mary has chosen the better part, which will not be taken away from her."

—LUKE 10:38-42

We can imagine how excited Martha was that Jesus accepted her offer to come to her home and spend some time with her. Martha was comfortable with hospitality, although she gave in to anxiety about the details of preparing a meal. Mary, on the other hand, seized the moment to be present to Jesus—to listen, respond, and share her heart with him.

We can learn from each of these women—from

Martha's openness to hospitality and Mary's example of being present to those we invite into our homes and seeing Christ in them. We can ask ourselves what we can do in order to better serve those who visit our homes. Are there things we need to let go of in order to be more hospitable?

Our Father delights in using the setting of a home to build up his people. There he can refresh and renew them. As we see Christ in every guest, the Holy Spirit is at work in ways we may never know.

A pastor of a parish tells his story: "I am often invited to homes for dinner. I enjoy getting to know people in this way. There is a family that stands out in my mind when it comes to being hospitable. When I enter their home, there is a particular atmosphere of peace, and conversation flows easily there. They want to know how my family is, how I am doing. They take a genuine interest in what is going on in my life. I always leave their home refreshed. There I experience being cared for, being listened to."

Father, as I age, regardless of circumstances, I want to learn to be more hospitable. Show me what I need to change in order to be freer to love others. ___

Making Adjustments

Statistics show us that an increasing number of aging adults are choosing to live in assisted-living situations. In some cases, this is the best decision. However, in other cases, the larger family prospers from the presence of aging members, as they bring gifts of love, faith, and family history.

Several years ago, a family of three generations gathered for their annual Christmas sing-along, a heartfelt and long-standing tradition that everyone enjoys. Afterward the adult children gathered to begin a conversation about their aging parents, who had been experiencing some recurring health issues.

Carlos and Marijane had hoped to live in their townhome until they passed on, but it had become increasingly difficult for their children to care for them. One daughter, Maria, and her husband, John, were most able to invite their parents to join them in their home. Carlos and Marijane accepted their offer to move in. Since this daughter lived close by, they could keep their doctors and go to the same church. With the extended family's help, they put their home up for sale, and it sold within two months.

Carlos says that he and Marijane have had to adjust

to giving up their driver's licenses and allowing their daughter to administer their medications. The loss of independence has been difficult but has been well compensated by the love and welcome their daughter and son-in-law have shown them. Marijane adds, "When I am having a rough day, I remember what my daughter said shortly after we arrived: 'I still can't believe we are the ones that got you!'"

Carlos lovingly describes how "it's a hard thing" for four strong personalities to live in the same home. However, they have all agreed to make every effort to live together peacefully. They enjoy shared meals, family celebrations, and frequent visits by the grandchildren. All of this provides a wonderful exchange of love.

Carlos and Marijane summed up this new season in life with one word: acceptance. "We realize we are helping one another work out our salvation" (see Philippians 2:12).

Many of us will come to a point at which we need to choose where we want to live out the later season of our lives. Prayer, careful consideration, and conversation with those close to us will yield peace.

Father, your love makes all things possible. Help me listen more carefully for your voice and recognize when you are acting in my life. ⸺

Wellness in Aging

Many studies show that socialization and ongoing education are important parts of aging well. Chances are, we will need to look for opportunities to spend time with friends and to avail ourselves of activities offered in our parish, at local senior centers, and through county programs.

We all need both fellowship and ongoing education as we age. But often we have to be intentional about staying connected with friends, sharing life with them, and continuing to learn new things. Visiting museums and historical landmarks, attending lectures and plays— even at the local high school, where they are affordable to most—are examples of activities that can help us continue learning and enjoying friends.

Another idea is to make a pilgrimage or enjoy a mini-retreat for a few hours. There are many places for this, from coast to coast. If we can't visit a sacred place, perhaps we can find a place to pray in a natural setting conducive to prayer. We can grow in our appreciation of the beauty of God's creation when we visit a rose garden in a local county park or take a short walk on a winding path.

One blustery, cold winter day, I gathered with some friends inside a warm church hall. Last-minute preparations were being made for a hot lunch. The round tables were set with white tablecloths, and large glass containers held decorative rocks and glittering candles. This senior luncheon featured a local internist, who would present a talk on wellness in aging.

There was plenty of time for fellowship before starting our lunch; the room was buzzing with conversation and laughter. The talk given by the doctor was practical, informative, and encouraging. It motivated me: the next week, I started preparing more fresh vegetables and serving fewer carbohydrates for dinner!

Inviting a friend to share such experiences with us is often God's way of spreading his love and delight among us. It is also an opportunity to get to know our friends better and thus be able to love and support them more effectively.

Father, I am overwhelmed with your generosity and your creative presence within and around me. Help me to be generous in spirit toward others as you guide me by your Holy Spirit. ⏤

Desires of the Heart

In our culture, we can sometimes forget where our true worth lies. We are inclined to measure our worth by what we achieve. But as we age and our strength and productivity decrease, we may find new purpose in the love and respect we show others.

Sunday was a special day of the week for Jimmie, a widow for sixteen years. After attending a church service, she would enjoy a warm meal with her family. Later she would guide them from her wheelchair through the halls of the nursing home where she lived.

Jimmie might pause at the entrance of a room and lovingly point to a woman lying in bed. The woman would greet her warmly with open arms, and they would exchange smiles. Jimmie would hold her hand over her heart and point upward with a look of great expectation. She had brought her family into this room to verbally pray for her friend and to console her with their words, something she could not do.

Nine years before, Jimmie had suffered a serious stroke, leaving an articulate, loving, and wise woman with only six words she could speak. Now she relied on the heartfelt words of her family to encourage others as they prayed together.

Jimmie had many friends to visit in her home, and her family would make the rounds with her. Many prayers were answered over time: family matters, deeper understanding for a person in need, reconciliations, courage in the face of limitations, and trust in God when facing death.

Jimmie had found peace and new meaning for her life. She had always been a prayerful woman. After working through the losses that accompanied the stroke, she realized that she could still reach others with the compassion of Christ. At times she just needed a little help from family members to verbalize what she could not. Jimmie knew that the Holy Spirit was working within and through her to bring comfort and hope to many. I know, because Jimmie was my precious mother.

I believe that deep down, the desire of our hearts is to live a life of grace, giving to others despite our limitations and sufferings. As we continue to pray to our Father, we can embrace his love and receive the gifts he gives us to bless others.

Father, as I age, may I decrease and may you increase within me, for your honor and glory. ⟶

Making Room in Our Hearts

Decluttering usually goes to the bottom of our list of what we would care to talk about, much less do. Few of us enjoy spending precious time going through stacks of paper or "stuff," much less clothing that doesn't fit anymore or was in style fifteen years ago.

Clutter can accumulate almost any place—the garage, the basement, closets, desks, and even chairs covered over by a pretty throw. (I know because I have one!) We may be reluctant to part with objects that we have collected over time or that were given to us by a loved one. Often these have sentimental value.

Numerous articles have been written on the topic of decluttering, and new ideas can help us get started. However, in the end, it usually takes something very important or pressing to motivate us to declutter successfully. We may have decided to downsize our home. There can be health issues. Or we may want to make more room in order to offer hospitality.

We need to remember that we are members of the body of Christ and that our Lord gives us a desire to be close to him and share in his life, his work, and his love, even as we get older. He proclaims that even in old age, we will bear fruit (see Psalm 92:14). As we come closer to the time when we will see Jesus face-to-face, he wants to protect our hearts so that we can continue to receive his love and give it to others.

Archbishop Fulton Sheen used to advise, "You must remember to love people and use things, rather than to love things and use people." Jesus knew the trap of things becoming treasures for us, and he encouraged us not to store up for ourselves treasures on earth but rather to store up treasures in heaven (see Matthew 6:19-21).

Warnings like these are helpful as we talk to the Lord in prayer about how we might simplify our lives and stay true to our relationship with him. Decluttering is one of those positive things we can do in order to put ourselves in a position to be more generous toward our Lord and others.

Father, draw me by your love to open my heart more fully to you, so that I may store up treasures for heaven and not for earth. —

Temples of the Holy Spirit

Most of the changes that occur in our bodies as we age occur slowly. From day to day, we may barely notice slight declines in our muscle tone, our joints, our memory, our sight, or our hearing. Cumulatively, however, these declines have an effect.

The good news is that there is much information today on how we can compensate for the normal changes that happen with age. Unfortunately, we may lack the desire to exercise, learn more about the brain, or pursue good nutrition.

Yet the truth is that our bodies are temples of the Holy Spirit (see 1 Corinthians 6:19-20). Now, that just might get our attention! As St. Paul reminds us, we are no longer our own. We have been bought at a price; therefore we honor God with our bodies (verse 20).

We should all consider how we might honor God with our bodies. What can we do to take better care of ourselves, so as to continue building up the body of Christ, however we are called to do so?

Bernice turned ninety-three this past year. She still lives in her home, but she is fortunate to have her son living in an apartment attached to the main house. She says, "I am still alive for a reason; God has plans for me to complete. It is important for me to cooperate with him."

Bernice has found that she keeps her hands flexible by doing a number of finger gymnastics early in the day. Folding laundry, dusting, and running the vacuum also help her to keep moving. She even cuts her own hair and then washes and styles it. She prays throughout the day and is inspired by the Holy Spirit to keep up with family and friends by writing notes of encouragement.

As I look to the future, I am encouraged by Bernice's commitment to keep herself moving, invested in life, and responding to the grace of the moment to love others with God's love.

Father, I need to receive more grace as I age. There are times when I can become discouraged because of illness, physical limitations, or just aches and pains. Help me to realize that because my body is the temple of your Holy Spirit, you care and are involved in encouraging me to take care of myself. What more can I do to cooperate with your grace? ___

Staying Engaged

Judith Martin, a nationally syndicated columnist, is better known as "Miss Manners" to her many followers. She gives timeless advice to people across the nation and has many loyal fans. She has also written numerous best-selling books on etiquette and society.

I had the opportunity to hear her speak at an Aging Fair several years ago. She was a gracious woman, lively and witty in her presentation. It was obvious that she was comfortable with the process of aging and was enjoying this season of life.

One thing she encouraged the seniors at the talk to do was to engage others. Referring to the art of conversation, she said, "Be as interested in another's opinion as you are in your own." She also talked about empathy and the importance of continuing to develop this gift throughout our lives.

Ed and Evelyn are in their early seventies. They both live with chronic illness; suffering is part of their lives. There are days when going out to spend time with others is difficult. Yet they remain deeply engaged with their family, friends, and those they serve.

They are Eucharistic ministers at the local hospital and nursing home. They continue to plan yearly extended family reunions, helping to keep the family connected as it grows. They also host weekly Sunday night dinners at their home for their son, Ed, his wife, Tina, and their four children. They realize that this is their opportunity to pass along valuable gifts, including their faith. It also gives the grandchildren a time to express their opinions and enter into lively conversations that span three generations!

Think about the conversations you have with friends and family, as well as with neighbors and people at your parish. Do you ask questions? Do you show interest in what others are doing? How can you develop more empathy for those you come in contact with?

As with Ed and Evelyn, it's important for us as we age to seek opportunities to engage with others. Continuing to develop the art of conversation and to grow in empathy, we will deepen our relationships and find new meaning and purpose in our lives.

Father, thank you for all the people in my life. Help me to stay engaged, even when I'm not feeling well. Give me fresh insight and wisdom to understand what I can do for others that would delight your heart and mine. —

Distractions

One beautiful, clear summer morning in July, I was sitting on the patio praying. I was focused on a particular verse in Scripture, listening to the words of truth about the love Jesus has for us and responding with deep gratitude. Suddenly, I was aware of something moving around my feet. When I looked down, I saw a cute little chipmunk. "No big deal," I thought. "He's harmless."

Focusing again on Scripture and trying to continue my litany of praise, I was aware of more movement inches away from my toes. Looking down again, I saw not one but three of these critters, not so cute by now because I know they have very sharp teeth! I picked up my things and went inside. I did not want to be distracted any longer, and I didn't want to leave my feet in harm's way!

This incident made me think about the distractions in my life and how they often get in the way of my good intentions, like praying or doing what needs to be done. I remembered two particular shirts belonging to my husband, still hanging in the closet because they needed to be mended. I *enjoy* mending, but I had let distractions keep me from doing the task. So my husband hadn't been able to wear those two shirts.

A wise priest once said, "Becoming so busy that we don't do the things God has planned for us is the sin of sloth." And so it goes with other distractions that we have given in to over time, eroding our good intentions.

Even our time in prayer with the Lord, when we often get the inspiration to love others, can be cut short or doesn't happen at all because of the distractions we experience. And just because, at this time in our lives, we might have more time to choose what we will do doesn't guarantee we will choose well. Let's ask for the grace to tame the distractions in our lives!

Lord, you know me well, even better than I know myself. You long for me to know the depth of your love and to experience your love working within me more fully. You see the subtleties that can distract me and keep me from yielding to your loving embrace. Shine your holy light on the things that erode my relationship with you and others. I want to receive more of your grace to live a life of love. ⸺

A Joyful Countenance

Have you ever had an unexpected meeting with someone that gave you a deeper insight into God's amazing love?

One of the traditions I enjoy with my daughter-in-law, Mary, while on vacation is picking a day to go to morning Mass, have lunch, and then go shopping. This year we ended up having a conversation after Mass with a man named Dennis.

A joy-filled man of eighty-two, Dennis was raised Catholic. He told us that as a young person, he had left the Church for some time. During those years, Dennis remembered, on three occasions he experienced inner promptings to "come back home." Finally he did. Over time he found that he was able to deal with many changes and trials because of God's grace.

One long-standing trial later in life was caring for his wife after she had a stroke. He eventually took an early retirement so that he could care for her full-time. At times his sorrow would become so great that he would walk out of his house and raise his hands and voice to God, asking, "Why, God, why us?" Dennis said he would finally yield to the loving presence of the Holy Spirit, who would calm his heart and mind. Reassured with divine confidence and love, he would return to his wife's side to serve her.

Dennis cared for his wife for eighteen years, until she passed away. Dennis said that without God's mercy and grace, he could never have lived a life of joy and victory in the midst of this trial.

I realized this chance meeting was God ordained. Mary's father, Ed, had cared for her mother, Louise, for many years. Like Dennis, Ed could never have endured the years that Louise suffered without God's generous help. Ed, too, served Louise with joy until the day she died. Our conversation with Dennis gave both Mary and me greater gratitude to our Lord, for both his personal interest in us and his action in our families.

Do you recall a time in your life when you were struggling and experienced God's intimate love for you? He is always waiting to embrace you, to console you, and to empower you to face whatever is ahead.

Father, regardless of what trials I may endure, you promise that you will never leave me or forsake me. I embrace your love and the gifts you give me in this season of my life.

Banishing Fear

Have you ever been concerned about being disabled in some way as you age? Has that concern caused you to be fearful? If so, have you thought you could do something about it?

Aunt Jennie believed in preparing for the future while trying to live well in the present. She had lived through World War I, the Great Depression, and World War II, witnessing much hardship and suffering. Jennie and her husband, Charles, were active in their church and supported others in their neighborhood when they could. However, because of health issues involving her eyes, Jennie was concerned that she might lose her sight as she aged.

When she was in midlife, she chose crocheting as her main hobby. Eventually, she could do her handiwork with great speed, even with her eyes closed. She donated the many beautiful pieces she crocheted to the nearby widows' and orphans' home, to sell at its bazaars. She lost her eyesight in her late seventies, but her ability to crochet would be put to good use for many more years. She died at the age of ninety-eight!

I will never forget my last visit with my dear Aunt Jennie, in 1964. I had taken my fiancé, Frank, to meet her. We had a lively conversation while Aunt Jennie crocheted with great speed, asking thoughtful questions in the process. She was so happy to meet Frank, sensing his kindness and our love for one another. As our visit ended, she handed me a gift of love: several intricately designed pot holders that she had crocheted.

Fifty years later, I still have one of the pot holders, a reminder of Aunt Jennie's resourcefulness and her love for God and others. "Whatever you do, work at it with all your heart, as working for the Lord, not for human masters, since you know that you will receive an inheritance from the Lord as a reward" (Colossians 3:23-24, NIV).

Aunt Jennie, like most of us, had concerns about aging and the debilitating changes it can bring. Rather than allowing fear to consume her, she worked hard at developing a gift to share with others despite her handicap.

Lord, you know what concerns I have about the future. Help me to work through them with great hope, no matter what the circumstances may be. ⸺

Trusting in His Promise

As we age, we might think about the possibility of one day having to travel our journey alone. Perhaps we are even faced with the prospect of dying alone.

Do you remember the song "You'll Never Walk Alone"? Richard Rodgers and Oscar Hammerstein wrote this song for the musical *Carousel*, first performed in 1945. World War II was ending, and many people had broken hearts. Loved ones did not come home from the war, and some families were torn apart. The future was unpredictable for many.

This musical came out at just the right time! People could set aside their heartaches and concerns for a time and get lost in the uplifting theme and music of the film, even if the story line didn't match the reality of their lives. People needed hope for the future, hope that no matter what happened, they would not be alone. They connected with the lyrics of the song, which went on to be recorded by many popular singers over the next three decades. The song amazingly stayed on the Top Ten chart for the next ten years!

The song is about perseverance—persevering through life's trials. Although it was not exactly written from a Christian point of view, the lyrics capture the longing of human hearts. We were created to belong, to be connected in soul and spirit to our Creator. The band Point of Grace sang "You Will Never Walk Alone" to underscore the promise that God has made to us: "Do not fear, for I am with you" (Isaiah 43:5).

As we advance in years, it is important to remember that God never intended us to travel this or any part of our journey alone. None of us knows what the future holds, but we do know who holds the future: God our Father. And he pursues us for deeper friendship. His desire is that we share life with him, connected to his body, the body of Christ—our family, our friends, and the other people he places in our lives. He has purpose for our lives: he wants us to embrace his love and share it with others—to support, strengthen, and affirm them in their relationship with the living God!

Father, your promises are true. You will never leave me or forsake me. Help me experience new freedom to believe in your purpose for my life until I see you face-to-face. —

The Gift of the Saints

Through Scripture and the accounts of saints, we come to know individuals who have said yes to God. Many of these saints overcame incredible roadblocks to remain faithful to God, even to the point of martyrdom.

St. Maximilian Kolbe was one of those saints who left us a legacy of faithfulness and love for God. As a young boy in Poland, he would stop in the local church and pray before going to the park to play. One time while he was praying, a woman appeared to him holding two crowns: one red, the other white. She told him that the red one stood for martyrdom, and the white one, for a life of purity. She asked him which one he would choose, and he chose both!

As a young man, Kolbe joined the Franciscans and was ordained. He worked tirelessly to print materials about Christ, the Church, Mother Mary, and the power of praying the Rosary. In 1941 Fr. Kolbe was seized by the Nazis and sent to Auschwitz.

One day a prisoner escaped, and ten men were chosen to die by starvation. This was a technique the Nazis used to deter additional escape attempts. One of the ten men in line cried out, "My wife! My children!" Fr.

Kolbe said, "I will take his place." The guards asked, "Who are you?" He simply answered, "I am a priest."

Fr. Kolbe spent his last days teaching the men in the starvation bunker about Christ and singing songs of thanksgiving with them. In the end, he was the last one alive, and he was given a lethal injection. Like Jesus on the cross of Calvary, he willingly and courageously laid down his life to save another.

The saints are great gifts to us. They show us that it is possible to say yes to God, no matter what the cost. We probably won't ever be asked to die for the sake of another person, but we are asked daily to die to our own needs so that we can help another person whose need might be greater. And when we find that difficult, we can ask the saints in heaven to intercede for us before our heavenly Father.

Jesus, you said there is no greater love than to lay down one's life for one's friends (John 15:13). Let me look for opportunities today to lay aside my own needs in order to serve someone else.

The Challenges of Life

It is easy to be joyful when all is going well, when we are in good health and our family is at peace. Yet the reality of life is that there are ups and downs, including sickness, disappointments, and trials. We live in an imperfect world, and we ourselves have many imperfections. How we handle these challenges says a lot about who we really are and how much we rely on Jesus to give us wisdom and insight.

As we read Scripture, we are invited into a new way of looking at trials. "My brothers and sisters, whenever you face trials of any kind, consider it nothing but joy, because you know that the testing of your faith produces endurance; and let endurance have its full effect, so that you may be mature and complete, lacking in nothing" (James 1:2-4).

Who of us, on our own, would count it "nothing but joy" when we are involved with a trial? Would we realize that the testing of our faith could produce endurance, and would we let endurance come to full perfection so that we might be fully mature and lacking in nothing? That is a radical stance to take, as radical as Jesus was to the culture of his time. His truth is countercultural.

Jesus exhorts us to not lose heart when we face trials of whatever kind. Instead, he invites us into a whole new way of thinking. He wants us to encounter him in the midst of a trial. As we take his invitation to heart and make it our own, we can freely choose to trust Jesus more. In the midst of trials, we can ask ourselves, "What is it that he wants me to do today? What choices can I make in order to place more of my trust in him?"

Jesus came to set us free to live a new life, to be transformed as we allow his grace, wisdom, and word to influence us. This transformation within us will happen one day at a time.

The good news is that the challenges we face can help to transform us as we find new meaning in life and greater purpose in Christ. This is God's plan, so let us encourage one another as we continue our journey.

Jesus, you make all things new. Continue to transform me into your image and likeness. ⸺

Celebrations

Our family had just finished celebrating our grandson Matthew's fifth birthday. We had shared a meal, put candles on the cake, and sung to him, and he had opened some gifts. I told him how special he was to all of us, and then I looked at him and asked, "Matthew, if you could ask Jesus for anything, what would it be?" He paused and said with a big smile, "Grammy, I would just thank him for life and love."

Have you ever stopped to think about what our lives would be like if we had nothing to celebrate? Celebrations are an integral part of our lives, and young Matthew's response reminded me of a valuable truth: the importance of building gratitude into all of our celebrations. It can become all too easy to forget the giver of all good gifts, our Father in heaven. Sometimes we need gentle reminders.

Our relationships with our children, grandchildren, nieces, and nephews open the door for us to make our celebrations truly memorable. For example, birthdays are wonderful times to express our love and gratitude to the person we are celebrating. Perhaps we can offer a prayer or take turns honoring the person by expressing how he or she has blessed us this year.

Thanksgiving is a natural opportunity to express our gratitude. Many families spend some time at the table mentioning something that they are especially grateful for that year.

We have treasured family traditions for celebrating religious holidays like Christmas and Easter. When my children were young, I baked a birthday cake for Baby Jesus for Christmas Day. Our tradition was to sing "Happy Birthday" to him early in the morning. It was a way to show our children that we rejoice, not because of the presents under the tree, but because of the gift of God's Son, Jesus.

Memorial Day, Independence Day, Labor Day, and Veterans Day—all offer opportunities for expressing gratitude to God for his goodness and mercy throughout our nation's history. We give thanks for those who have given their lives to protect America and for the freedom we share as a people.

What memories do you have of celebrations that were special? Who has inspired you to be grateful?

Father, thank you for the gift of celebrations. Help me to have a heart of gratitude and love and to share it with others as we gather together. ⸺

Being Present to Our Families

How very good and pleasant it is
when kindred live together in unity!
—Psalm 133:1

Having grandchildren is a blessing, and it gives us an opportunity to reflect God's love to someone over time. This commitment to love our grandchildren requires an investment not only of our hearts but of our time and resources as well.

My husband and I have always been long-distance grandparents, so we decided early on that we would try to be present when each grandchild was baptized, made their First Communion, was confirmed, and graduated from high school and college. We never dreamed we would be blessed with eleven grandchildren and, to date, one great-grandchild! It has meant a lot of travel, but each occasion has given us many opportunities to celebrate God's love and faithfulness with that child and the family.

When Greg, our firstborn grandchild, received his First Communion, he said to us, "Pop Pop and Grammy, you are always here when something important happens."

His insight and appreciation inspired us to continue to embrace the challenge of bridging the miles between us and do all we can to celebrate special events with our extended family.

Even if we are not able to be present at a home on the actual date of a birthday, we find a time to celebrate later, such as when we are with the family on vacation or a holiday weekend. Our commitment to be invested in our grandchildren's lives by being present to them in these important moments has been one of the best ways we've found to share our love with them.

Greg graduated from college and has since been serving as an army officer. He brought his sweetheart, Monica, to meet us before they were engaged. They stayed with us for several days, and it was easy to see why he loved her so much. After they were married and their little girl, Sofia, was born, they made a commitment to travel across the country to attend a family reunion. I could only thank God for Greg and his family and for everyone who made the trip. Their very presence expressed their love for one another.

Jesus, thank you for my family. Help me to reach out to each member and share your goodness and love with him or her. ⸺

The Door of God's Mercy

"No repentance is too late for the person who still remains in this world. The approach to God's mercy is open."[3] These words were spoken by St. Cyprian many centuries ago. And they are still true, even if we are sometimes tempted to give up praying for someone who is away from God and the Church.

It can be frustrating to pray for someone for a long time with no apparent results. However, if we continue to talk with God about the person, he will help us. Not only will he give us a desire to continue praying, but we may find in time that his desires for the person have become our desires!

One woman had been away from the Church—and from God—for more than thirty-five years. She had become cynical, hardened over time by personal disappointments, declining health, and loneliness. A friend who often visited her would share stories about how God had acted in various circumstances, but the woman did not show much of a response.

One day her friend asked her if she would like a Christian funeral someday. She replied, "Why would

I want that? I have lived my life the way I wanted to, and when I die, that is the end."

There was no reason to hope this woman's mind would change; in fact, over time she was becoming even more hardened and more depressed. However, her friend continued to pray for her conversion and asked close friends to pray as well. In time, the friend believed that she was experiencing God's own tenderness and his desires for the woman.

Then came a surprising turn of events. Over the next several visits, this woman became open to prayer, and she eventually said, "I would like to have the Anointing of the Sick given to me by a priest." A few months later, she asked to have her confession heard, and she received Communion. Our Father had poured out his mercy upon her for years, and over time he convinced her of his great love for her.

Our Father's love is consistent, relentless, passionate, and forgiving. He wants to use all of us to express his love and mercy to hurting people in the world today.

Father, help me to express your love and mercy to others, regardless of the circumstances.

God's Surprises

Are we aware that God is full of surprises? Are we afraid of what God might surprise us with? Here is how Pope Francis talks about God's surprises:

> *Newness* often makes us fearful, including the newness which God brings us, the newness which God asks of us. . . . We are afraid of God's surprises. Dear brothers and sisters, we are afraid of God's surprises! He always surprises us! The Lord is like that.[4]

We might remember the story of St. Teresa of Calcutta, who heard the calling at an early age to enter religious life. She became a Sister of Loreto at the age of eighteen and then worked in India as a high school teacher. Years later, in 1946, on a train journey from Calcutta to Darjeeling, Teresa received what she termed a "call within a call." God surprised her!

We can all be saints in the making, since God delights in sharing his love and his joy with us, often surprising us in the process. We just have to make time to listen to what he may be calling us to do.

Georgine had just retired from her position as

associate dean of nursing at a nearby university when her husband died rather suddenly. She had been thinking about starting a parish nursing program, but after becoming a widow, Georgine took some time to work through this unexpected loss. As she prayed, the Lord "surprised" Georgine by showing her that she should continue to move forward with her plans to become a parish nurse.

So she launched the program at her parish. She served the poor who had no access to health care by offering periodic health screenings, which became very popular. She also visited the homebound and supported caregivers with a monthly luncheon.

Georgine heard the voice of Jesus calling her to serve through the needs she saw in the parish. Surprised by the Lord, she found a new way of serving others, which gave her joy even while she was in the midst of grieving.

We may be entering a new season in our lives. What surprises does God have for us? How can we listen to his still, small voice? He may reassure us, give us a helpful insight, or even inspire us to share his love in a new way.

Father, I thank you for all the ways your love has changed my life, bringing me joy. Help me to trust you more. ⸺

A Blessed Encounter

Perhaps you have heard the saying "There are no atheists in foxholes." Most people, when death seems imminent, will try to turn to God. Some want to bargain so they can be helped; others try to find peace.

There are many stories of deathbed conversions in hospitals and nursing homes. However, there are no guarantees that any of us will be in a position to avail ourselves of God's mercy at the time of death. Death can come suddenly, when we least expect it. Pope Francis has reminded us, "It is the favorable time to heal wounds, . . . a time to offer everyone, everyone, the way of forgiveness and reconciliation."[5]

Being aware of how generous God is in pouring out his love and mercy should encourage us to live more fully in the power of the Holy Spirit. Otherwise we can underestimate our ability to help someone come back to Christ. We might know what to say to a hurting person but fail to speak because we fear putting up a wall between us.

Paul was retired from the army and was in a military hospital waiting for exploratory surgery to determine the source of his intestinal pain. His roommate, Frank, was there for surgery as well. A priest came in to bring Communion to both of them, but only Frank received. After the priest left, Frank asked, "Why didn't you receive Communion?"

Paul said he had been away from the Church for thirty years. "I had a very bad experience in the confessional and never went back."

Frank said, "It is not too late to come back. The priest here could help you."

Paul answered, "No."

Frank leaned forward and spoke with compassion. "Paul, this is a different priest—I know him. He won't scold you, but like Christ, he will welcome you back with open arms."

Paul changed his mind and found the priest. After his confession, he told Frank, "I never had such a wonderful experience. I'm forgiven!"

The next day, Paul received bad news: he had cancer, and he had only a short time to live. Yet Paul was at peace. He had reconciled with God and the Church, and he died a happy man.

Father, you can do far more through me than I can imagine. Your love for others grows in me the more I reach out to help them. ⌒

God's Timing

God wants us to spend time each day with him in prayer so that we are led by the Spirit to do his will. This can bear great fruit, not only for us, but for others as well.

One morning Beth was praying, and her neighbor came to mind. As she continued to pray, she had a desire to visit her neighbor that morning. The time was not convenient, but she stopped by Judy's home on the way to an appointment.

When Judy opened the door, Beth could see that she looked very sad. Judy asked if Beth could come in and have a cup of coffee. Beth agreed, and the two talked for a while. Finally, Judy broke down in tears.

Judy and her husband had two children, and she was pregnant with their third child. Her husband had told her that if she did not get an abortion, he was going to divorce her. The abortion was going to take place the very next day.

Beth was shocked and deeply saddened by the news. As the two talked more about the gift of life within her, Beth felt strengthened by the Holy Spirit. She prayed with Judy that she would make the right decision. She also urged Judy to pray fervently over the next twenty-four hours for the Lord's will to be done. Judy needed great love and courage to stand her ground for life. The two stayed in close touch that night.

By the next day, Judy had made a decision for life. She would keep her baby. God was with her! He had filled her with his Spirit and strengthened her to stand with him.

Judy's husband kept his promise and moved out. Six months later, Judy gave birth to a healthy, beautiful baby boy. With God's help and the support of family and friends, Judy carried on. Eventually, she moved to another state to be close to her parents and extended family.

One Saturday some ten years later, there was a knock on Beth's door. Standing there was Judy with a strong, handsome boy by her side. They had returned for a surprise visit. Judy wanted to thank Beth for getting involved in helping to save her son's life. The three of them celebrated together!

Father, I want to be more involved in sharing your love with others. Come, Holy Spirit; strengthen and inspire me! —

Snail Mail

In 1942 the term "snail mail" appeared in the headlines of news articles about slow mail service. The term caught on and is still used today. Yet however slow the mail may be, one of the advantages of receiving letters, notes, and cards through the postal service is that it enables us to experience again and again things that otherwise could be forgotten.

Have you saved cards, picked out just for you and written with love? They can cheer you up on a day when you might feel lonely. Perhaps you have letters from your parents that have become part of your family history.

I found a pack of letters that my mother had kept, letters that she and my father had exchanged many years ago. It was during their courtship, from 1930 to 1932, when they wrote to one another every week. The letters are valuable to me. They express the things that were important to them: thoughts about their families, the qualities they loved in one another, the fears they had to work through, and their desire to be married and welcome children.

I have also kept a series of letters my husband and I exchanged while he served as an army officer in the

Vietnam War and in Cambodia. These letters hold a valuable part of our family history. I want my grandchildren to read them!

Another advantage of writing letters and notes is to affirm and encourage others. There was a bishop who was known for his commitment to answer within a month every personal note he received. After he died, many people came forward to witness to what he had done for them through his personal responses. He certainly built up the body of Christ through this simple courtesy!

As we age, we may be limited in our activities. It is important to develop new ways to stay connected to others, to take an active role in sharing the love of Christ. Sending notes, cards, and letters through the mail is one way to continue to let "our cup overflow" for the sake of others.

Jesus, thank you for being faithful to me in every season of my life. Help me to realize that everyone has needs and that I have an opportunity nearly every day to make a difference in someone's life. Here I am, Lord; use me. ——

Fostering Friendships

Friendship is truly a gift from the Lord, but all good relationships take some work and prayerful thought. How can we deepen our friendships and develop new ones?

One characteristic of friendship is the ability to have meaningful conversations with one another. Friends want to be able to discuss a variety of topics. As we age, we may sometimes be intimidated about entering into conversations, as our world of experience may be getting smaller. Here are things we can consider.

What things delighted me this past week? We could talk about a meal we prepared and enjoyed or about how our exercise program is going (or not going, for that matter). We could share about a good book we're reading or an interesting movie we saw. How did I see Christ at work this past week? What Scripture passage inspired me? What good things happened in my family?

One more thing to consider: when asking a friend about her day, it is better to ask, "What did you do today?" rather than "How are you?" The question "What did you do today?" will generate conversation!

Some time ago, a group of my friends asked what I would like to do for my birthday. I had some ideas, but mostly I wanted to get together and have each person bring a memory of a fun surprise that she had experienced. As we shared our stories, we all laughed hard. I loved the time we spent together, and I got to know each woman better!

I realized that I was not just learning new things about my friends. Something significant happens when a woman shares her life! We get to know who she is as a person. The more we learn about a friend, the more we are able to love her.

With that goes a responsibility to keep the personal things we learn about our friends confidential. How can trust and respect grow between friends if we gossip about one another? Perhaps we can agree to keep our conversations confidential unless someone is in serious trouble and needs professional help.

Jesus, you call me your friend, and you encourage me to be a better friend to others. Continue to inspire me to love others as you love me. ⌐

The Good News

Do you know who the patron saint of preachers is? You might think it is some famous priest or eloquent teacher who could persuade others and move the masses to repentance. Well, I was surprised to learn that it is Mary Magdalene, who was the first to see the risen Lord.

Jesus instructed Mary to tell the disciples the good news that he indeed was fully alive, risen from the dead, just as he had promised. Mary ran to tell the disciples. Discounting her obvious excitement, they did not believe her, and Peter and John ran to see for themselves.

Mary knew how much Jesus loved her. He had delivered her from seven demons (see Luke 8:2). That experience of freedom gave her a burning desire to follow him as his faithful disciple.

When have you experienced the fact that Jesus really loves you in a deep and personal way? If you have not yet had that experience, it is not too late. I encourage you to remain open and ask Jesus to do something new within you. This may include expressing sorrow for your sins and, if you are Catholic, using the confessional.

You can ask Jesus to enliven his Holy Spirit within you, helping you to recognize his voice more clearly.

He wants to reveal his love to you in new and deeper ways. He wants to fill you with his blessings and the gifts of his Holy Spirit. He wants you to be confident that he is with you, changing you and helping you to have even deeper trust in his love for you.

You, like Mary Magdalene, can experience the love and faithfulness of Jesus when you least expect it. You can be on the lookout for moments when you witness his love in action: another person having a breakthrough in faith, an answered prayer, some good news you read about, your heart being moved by mercy to forgive someone who has deeply hurt you, a child's hug, someone giving alms to a needy person. Then, like Mary Magdalene, you can hurry to tell someone around you the good news: Jesus is alive and changing hearts!

Jesus, I want to experience your love in a deeper way. I ask you to do something new within me. Then give me the eyes to see and the heart to share your love with others.

Amazing Grace

In the movie *Amazing Grace*, there is a touching moment when William Wilberforce takes a few minutes from his busy day to enjoy the beautiful outdoors. Running in a field, he decides to fall onto the damp grass, roll around, and look into the blue skies—all while dressed in the elaborate clothes of the late 1700s. Suddenly the butler appears and, after some conversation, asks him, "You found God, Sir?" Wilberforce replies with a broad grin, "I think he found me!"

As the story unfolds, it becomes clear that there is no way Wilberforce could have successfully fulfilled his purpose of abolishing the English slave trade without God's constant intervention in his life and without the help of others. Three of those people were his boyhood friend William Pitt, his wife, Barbara, and John Newton. God brought these people and others together for a great purpose, *his* purpose.

Newton at one time had been captain of a ship that transported people, under horrific conditions, to Europe to be sold as slaves. Newton referred to those men and women as the "twenty thousand ghosts" that constantly haunted him. He pleaded with Wilberforce to help bring an end to the English slave trade.

For twenty-eight years, Wilberforce struggled mightily in Parliament as a member of the House of Commons. Finally, he achieved his noble goal.

At times it is helpful for us to remember the people who have been influential in our lives. Whom did God use over the course of your life to teach, train, and mold you? Who taught you to show love or showed you the way to forgive—yourself and others? Maybe people came together with you to change a situation for good, even for God's honor and glory! Perhaps you could take some time to prayerfully consider all those who played a part in shaping your thoughts and beliefs and who you are today.

Newton wrote the hymn "Amazing Grace" to testify to his conversion. Have you ever thought of writing your own hymn, a legacy you will leave to family and friends? Your story can glorify God and witness to his everlasting faithfulness long after you have passed into eternal life.

Father, help me to consider how others have worked in my life and how you want to use me to encourage others. —

Faithfulness Day after Day

When we do the right thing day after day, we can see positive changes. For example, studying the value of good nutrition and putting that knowledge into practice daily can help improve our overall well-being. Being informed about the aging process and learning to adapt to the changes in our bodies and environment can help us welcome these years and be a blessing to others.

What about matters of the heart? We know that God is faithful, and if we respond to his promptings of love and encouragement day after day, we can become more faithful, loving, and encouraging. Being faithful to reading and praying with the Scriptures helps us know God's mind and what he might do in particular circumstances. Receiving the Eucharist on a regular basis empowers us to be merciful to others as God is merciful to us. Doing the right thing in these "matters of the heart" prepares us for situations that will test us.

Bill had a severe brain hemorrhage and died shortly afterward. He did not have a will or document that stated what he wanted the family to do with his body. Tension arose in the family as members met at the funeral home to decide whether to have the body cremated or embalmed.

For the next two days, one part of the family—Bill's mother, sister, brother, and brother-in-law—prayed consistently for wisdom. After praying throughout the second night, the mother discerned that it was God's will that she let go and give others the choice about Bill's remains.

During the "sign of peace" at the funeral Mass, God's mercy was evident. Family members who had yielded the right to choose how the body would be prepared for burial crossed the aisle. One by one they went down the pews, smiling and showing God's mercy and love. Later, at the reception, the two sides of the family talked pleasantly with one another and mingled with guests.

We never know what will be tested—our desires, our principles, our faith, how we treat others. Staying close to the Lord and open to the nudging of the Holy Spirit will help us discern God's will, even when the unexpected comes upon us.

Father, your faithfulness toward me brings me joy and peace. Help me be faithful in turn to the people in my life.

Miracle on Christmas Eve

Have you ever prayed for someone over a long period of time for a particular purpose? Sometimes when our faith is challenged, it grows, and hope grows too. After all, our faith is rooted in a person, the living God, who promises he will never leave us or forsake us. He will be close to us no matter what the circumstances are.

Mary Jane and Patrick relied on God's comfort when their son, Vincent, went to fight in World War II. Vincent wrote every week. In one letter, he said, "Our unit was crossing a field when we spotted a Messerschmitt fighter aircraft bearing down on us. We tried to get cover, but men on my right and on my left were killed instantly. My hair turned completely white within a few days."

All of a sudden, the letters stopped. A month passed, then another, then a few more. Finally, the family heard from the War Department: Vincent was missing in action. Faced with the bad news, the family would not give up. They rallied friends, parishioners, and neighbors to join them in praying for their missing son.

The Christmas season of 1944 approached, and the family wanted to keep things as normal as possible. The

Christmas tree was put up and decorated, and lights adorned the windows.

On Christmas Eve night, there was a knock at the door, followed by a loud commotion. The grandchildren ran into the living room and heard their grandparents saying, "The telegram says Vincent is fine; he was missing, and now he has been found!"

After the excitement died down, the family all earnestly prayed, thanking God for their Christmas Eve miracle. My husband, Frank, remembers this night very well: Vincent was his favorite uncle!

Months later Vincent returned home from the war. To the astonishment of all, he had no knowledge of the telegram or of who could have sent it.

This family's faith was tried, and through it, they grew closer to God and one another. Have you found deeper meaning in life as you trusted God for something important?

Father, I desire to have a closer relationship with you. I give you the circumstances in my life and the people I am close to. Help me trust you more and more. ⌐

When Love Runs Thin

It matters to God how we care for our family members and those who are in need. In fact, Jesus said to us, "A new command I give you: Love one another. As I have loved you, so you must love one another" (John 13:34, NIV).

There are times when loving another person is difficult. We can experience our love running thin and our willingness to continue giving drying up. Have you ever experienced this on some level?

Some years ago, I was helping to care for my mother, who had suffered a severe stroke. She was a total-care patient, and with the help of the nursing center where she lived, I was able to love her by attending to the little details that were so important to her. For eight years, we had a wonderful routine that met her needs and brought her much happiness. We took care of her personal belongings, did crafts together, and shared meals with friends. Then her health declined further, and she stopped eating. She was giving up.

I knew my mother needed me by her side for longer periods of time. I was torn; my family also needed me. And besides, there were times in the past when I really needed my mother, and she wasn't there for me. There it was, the greater obstacle: a hurt still harbored. I said, "God, I just can't give much more; my love is running thin."

I pictured our Lord with his arms wide open to me, and I ran to him by going to confession. I needed to let go of the hurt I had experienced as a teen; indeed, my mother had asked for forgiveness years earlier. After I let that hurt go and truly forgave her, I asked for God's grace to help me love her more deeply.

For many weeks, I spent hours by my mother's side. Eventually she started eating, her health improved, and we were blessed to have her with us for another year.

That was an important year. Our daughter, Tina, was married, and my mother was able to attend the wedding. Years earlier she had promised Tina she would be at her wedding someday, and God helped her fulfill that promise.

Father, your love heals all wounds. Continue to show me what to let go of so that I can love more deeply. —

Delighting God

Imagine that you were going to spend some time talking to one of your favorite people—perhaps a grandchild or another family member or a friend. You would look forward to that time. Then after your time spent together, you would savor the things that were shared and delight in the heartfelt connection.

What if the Holy Spirit put it on your heart to reach out to someone and make that kind of connection? God's Spirit often sends us out to others, to encourage them and give them hope when they need it. Let us think about that for a moment: God, so much a part of our lives, is living and dwelling within us. We could delight him by reaching out to someone who is on his heart!

My husband, Frank, and I were on vacation, and he was enjoying the slower pace of life. Early one morning, as the dawn was breaking, he decided to go for a walk on the beach. During the long walk, he found himself thanking God again and again for his love and generosity. As he headed back, he noticed a lone figure in the distance sitting by the water. Frank felt the Holy Spirit inspiring him to go over and say hello.

In a short while, the men were in conversation about the joys of being fellow Christians. As it turned out, Rufus was having some problems within his family, and he had come down to the water to think things over. Frank offered to pray with him, and the two men asked for God's help. As Rufus was leaving, he said to Frank, "Now I know why I came down to the water this morning."

How honored God was in that surprise meeting! Two people coming together to share about his goodness, the delight they experienced knowing he was in their midst, and their confidence in calling on him for help.

Perhaps you want to take a few minutes to remember all the times God's Spirit has inspired you to reach out to others. What has that been like for you? How did you feel when others reached out to you in a time of need?

Father, I thank you that you care about the details of my life and the lives of others. I thank you that your love has no fear. Help me to be more open to the inspiration of your Holy Spirit.

Saints among Us

Many of us have our favorite saints to call upon for special or seemingly impossible needs. Many of those prayers are answered over time. Saints can also inspire us, long after they have died and entered into the heavenly courts. Their lives have not ended, just changed, and at times they change our lives as well!

Fr. Damien de Veuster of Molokai is one saint who has inspired many people. His love for those with leprosy was so great that he accepted the assignment to live and work among them, knowing it probably meant a death sentence for him. After living among the sick, nursing them, tending to their spiritual and pastoral needs, caring for their children, and being present to the dying, he announced in 1885, "I am one of you." He had contracted leprosy, yet he continued to build clinics, churches, and a hospital, as well as more than six hundred coffins. He died among his people in 1889, at the age of forty-five, and was buried on Molokai.

Years later a Belgium bishop petitioned that Fr. Damien's body be exhumed and brought back to his hometown in Belgium. Among the crowds that day to welcome him home were two young people: Paul

Wynants, age eleven, and his sister, age thirteen. It was on that day that Paul and his sister received their first call to enter the religious life. Paul eventually became a Missionhurst priest, and his sister became a nun.

I first met Fr. Paul in 1979. He was serving as a chaplain at the local hospital. He had a gift of uniting people, bringing them a sense of community and letting them know that "I am one of you." In the same way that Fr. Damien cared for those who were sick, Fr. Paul cared for people in the hospital. He also encouraged and prayed with us Eucharistic ministers and taught us the importance of listening carefully to others.

Frank and I were blessed to visit with Fr. Paul shortly before he died. He was very weak but totally present to us. At the end of our conversation, he smiled and said, "God is showing us once again how much we need one another."

Father, your love is transparent in the lives of saints and holy people who surround me. Nourish my awareness of your delight in dwelling among us! ⸺

A Great Responsibility

Grandparents, who have received the blessing to
see their children's children (cf. Psalm 128:6), are
entrusted with a great responsibility: to transmit
their life experience, their family history, the history
of a community, of a people; to share wisdom with
simplicity, and the faith itself—the most precious
heritage! Happy is the family who have
grandparents close by!

—POPE FRANCIS[6]

Pope Francis knows our hearts. He knows that as we age, we grow weary and may wonder if we are still needed by the family. Yet when we have such thoughts, we can shift our focus and think about what is our God-given responsibility to our grandchildren. We as grandparents need to understand our value to the extended family, whether we live close by or not. We can seek ways of enhancing relationships by sharing our stories, our faith experiences, and our very presence with our grandchildren.

Being long-distance grandparents has challenged Frank and me to pray and be creative in sharing life with our grandchildren. Last year we had an unexpected opportunity to deepen our connection with an adult granddaughter, Shannon. This very loving and gifted young woman had finished two years of college and decided to take a break. She wasn't sure she wanted to continue in her current major or continue going to the same college. She was also trying to work through some problems that had been troubling her. She came to live with us, some five hundred miles from home. She got a job and began making some new friends. We had many opportunities to share our lives together.

We had some rough patches to work through, but we all relied on the abundant grace and love Jesus held out to us. After six months, Shannon returned home, and she is now enrolled in a different college with a different major. She is happy and doing well in her studies.

Our Father will continue to give you the gifts and grace you need as you share your life, your faith, and your stories with the generations after you.

Father, I desire to share your love more fully with my family. Help me to grow in understanding your role for me as I share my life with the next generation.

Finding Peace

We live in an age in which there are more and more medical options available to us, which certainly can be seen as God's blessings. There are times, however, when an illness is terminal and medical advances only prolong the pain and suffering. That is why it is important that we make our wishes known to our families in advance. Then we are free to focus our time and attention on God and on family members and friends close to us.

This includes making sure there are no hurts harbored or grudges held. We need to humble ourselves and let go of hurts. This was very important to Jesus, who told us to forgive others so that we can be forgiven (see Matthew 6:14). When we forgive or ask forgiveness of another, we are then set free to love more deeply!

I recently had lunch with a friend, Gladys. She survived a serious bout of cancer some ten years ago. She has spent these past years in quality time with her sons and their families as well as her friends. She has also been part of a Bible study, by which she has experienced a growing trust in God. She has struggled in letting go of some past hurts but is in the process of forgiving others.

Gladys recently found out that the cancer has returned. She is now eighty-six. After praying and talking with loved ones, she came to a peaceful decision: not to undergo chemo again but to live out her days trusting in God's timing. She is using the time she has left to put things in further order. Gladys is able to live alone and still serve a lovely lunch!

What decisions do you need to make to help you find deeper meaning in your life day by day? Perhaps it would be helpful to talk over the details with someone close to you or with a priest.

Father, I want to lighten my load, both externally and internally. I need your help in bringing to mind where I need to start. If there is anything that needs to be set right, please enlighten me. I want to spend my last days in peace, being present to you and others. ⸺

The Eye of the Storm

Have you ever been through a hurricane?

Some years ago, Frank and I were on vacation at the shore in North Carolina. He returned home to Virginia, to go back to work. A week later, some family members were coming to join me. In the meantime, I was without a car, which normally would have been fine. However, a hurricane out in the Atlantic suddenly took a turn toward the Carolinas. It was bearing down quickly, and it was a big one!

I was very frightened, and I was alone. I had to first think about closing down our home there, which was no small task. And then where would I go? What would be my safest port in this storm?

Before Frank and I could even talk about it, our friends Wayne and Debbie called and offered me a place in their home. They lived about twenty-five miles inland. Furthermore, they would drive down right away to get me and help close and secure the home. I was overwhelmed with God's gift to me through these dear friends!

The huge hurricane battered the North Carolina coastline for four straight days. We were fortunate to find ourselves in the "eye of the storm" during that time. On land the center of the eye is by far the calmest part of the storm, with skies mostly clear of clouds and with little wind and rain. At times a person in the eye can see blue skies during the day and stars at night. I was fortunate to experience that beautiful sight. The turbulence, chaos, and destruction, though right around us, did not affect us. It was an experience I will always remember, a sign of God's presence and beauty in the midst of uncertainties and dangers.

God our Father is our safe harbor, our sure refuge, our place of hope no matter what is going on around us. In fact, even in the midst of life's uncertainties and trials, something beautiful can happen if we stay close to him, in the center of his love, relying on his presence to accompany us through each and every storm we face.

Father, your gift to me is your ability to be present no matter what is going on in my life. Teach me to be more aware of your presence every day. ——

"Grammy Jokes"

We can learn a lot about our loved ones as we experience simple pleasures with them. With a little creativity and inspiration, we can be purposeful in giving a gift of joy at family gatherings. Sometimes our ideas are a hit; other times we learn not to repeat them!

I remember well when Frank and I started taking vacations with our children and grandchildren. At the time, there were only three grandchildren, ages six, four, and eighteen months. I wanted to give a break to our son, Mark, and his wife, Mary, so I carefully planned some crafts to do with the children. I thought we could collect shells and then glue them onto small Styrofoam wreaths.

To make a long story short, the wreaths, without the shells, ended up on the heads of the two older children, making the baby laugh at the sight of them! We resorted to coloring. To this day the family laughs at the photo, now hanging in a large collage, of the kids from twenty-one years earlier with wreaths on their heads.

We didn't give up trying to create fun for the children on vacations. We learned to think and plan together, leaving lots of time for just letting things happen.

Stopping at ice cream stands, playing games, doing puzzles, riding the waves, and learning to fish—all have been big-time hits over the years.

Our family grew; eventually, we would sit down to dinner with six adults and eleven children. We all looked forward to dinner together, but I must admit that the numbers were daunting, with everyone crammed around one large table! It was then that I thought of having a few jokes to tell the kids during dinner. Never did I anticipate how that would catch on.

Right after we said grace, the chant would begin among the children, led by Joe, Mary Claire, Colin, and Mae: "Grammy jokes, Grammy jokes, Grammy jokes!" The kids only got louder until I told a joke. Much laughter and fun followed. Then they would tell some of their own jokes. (These were very corny on both sides!) Even now, some of our grandchildren who are in their twenties will ask for a Grammy Joke. We all need a little levity at times!

What simple pleasures have you experienced with your family or another family? What gift of yourself can you share?

Father, you give me the gift of creativity. Help me to show love to someone today. ⌒

Hope for the Future

As the years pass and we grow older, we can be tempted to look at the future with some trepidation. After all, we may reach a point someday when we are not able to care for ourselves. What will life look like when that time arrives?

Our fears are compounded by the fact that in our culture today, the elderly are not honored and cherished as they once were. Families are often separated by many miles, and a lack of personal contact can cause relationships to fray. In some cases, when parents become too old to live alone, they are left to work out their living situation by themselves.

Linda was in shock when her husband of sixty-five years died suddenly of a heart attack. For years they had cared for one another in their home, assisted by someone several times a week. They were able to remain independent up to that point in life, and then, overnight, everything changed.

After the funeral, Linda's sons and daughter came together to talk about what the future might look like for Linda. She was in her eighties and could not live alone. Her personal desire was to stay in her home, but how could that happen? She wasn't able to hire help twenty-four hours a day.

Then a son and his wife offered to sell their home and move in with Linda. Jacqueline was a professor at a nearby college, so she would be close by during the day, and David's office wasn't too far away either. A nurse's aide could come several times a week to assist Linda, and later they would increase the assistance to daily.

Jacqueline and David lived with Linda for fifteen years, honoring her and learning much from her during that time. The compassion that this son and his wife extended to Linda touched many lives during that time and beyond.

We don't know what the future holds or how our living situations will change in time. But while none of us knows what the future holds, we all know who holds the future: God our Father! As we grow in trust in his providence and care, we will be able to weather whatever he has in store for us.

Father, help me to embrace you with love and with gratitude for the compassionate ways you have cared for me. ⎯

A Little Bit of Heaven

Each Sunday we join in the celebration of the Mass, when our Lord feeds us with his Body and Blood. We look forward to the celebration that is even now going on in heaven, with all of our brothers and sisters in Christ who are united forever with God. Yet even our earthly celebrations can reflect the joy of heaven, when family and friends gather together and rejoice in one another.

That is exactly what I experienced as we celebrated our fiftieth wedding anniversary three summers ago. Initially I was reluctant to go forward with the preparations. My husband, Frank, convinced me to just enjoy the process. He wrote me a beautiful letter expressing his love for me and pointing out that this could be the last big thing he could do for me. How could I say no to that?

The family all pitched in to plan the party, and finally our special night arrived. We gathered in our parish church for Mass, which was followed by an anniversary blessing by our wonderful pastor. That was a very special moment for me, as I looked around to see so many of our family and friends standing with us. There we were, in the autumn of our lives, thankful to God for his faithfulness through the good as well as the difficult times. God's love had enabled us to be present to renew our commitment of love to one another, with family and friends present.

At one point during the party, I was dancing with one of my grandsons, Patrick. He looked endearingly at me and asked, "So, Grammy, what is your favorite part of this evening?" Immediately I said, "Right now it is dancing with you, Patrick!" I then added, "I think tonight is a bit of what heaven will be like, surrounded by family and friends, experiencing so much of God's love."

Celebrations are an important part of our lives, and as we age, they become even more poignant—including past ones. Recall some of the celebrations in your own life. What was special about them? Perhaps you can enjoy getting out photo albums and thanking the Lord for these moments. Think about some of the gifts God is giving you today, in this season of your life, that you would like to celebrate with others.

Father, I am overwhelmed at times with your love. Help me to celebrate all the gifts you have for me. ⁓

A Caring Attitude

As we age, most of us long for greater meaning and depth in our lives. We want to be more sincere and caring. How we are present to others can open the door for true caring. The following story illustrates one example of what that open door can look like.

For years Tony had gone to daily Mass at our parish. He was a weekday lector and would faithfully fill in for lectors who were absent. After Mass he would linger outside to talk with those who had a minute. He was always interested in how you and your family were doing, and over time he would follow up to see how things had turned out.

One day after Mass, Tony walked outside and said he wasn't feeling well. Within moments he collapsed. The priest acted quickly and gave him the Anointing of the Sick, after which Tony was taken to the hospital, where his wife and daughter met him. A short time later, Tony died.

On the day of the funeral, many came to honor this humble man, and many delightful stories about Tony came to light. He had made it a habit to record the prayer requests that people gave him after Mass. Then during the night, when he couldn't sleep, he would pick up his book and begin interceding for those needs.

Using his connections in the business world, Tony would help those who were unemployed search for jobs. He also made it a habit to visit the sick in the parish, sitting with them and listening with great love and interest. His kind smile and ready wit helped soothe many a troubled heart.

In his book *After 50: Spiritually Embracing Your Own Wisdom Years*, Dr. Robert J. Wicks says,

> [A] caring attitude also, at its very core, involves embracing a special kind of *willingness*. By that I mean:
> —A willingness to *listen*;
> —A willingness to *be open*; and
> —A willingness to *be faithful*.
> All three serve to enrich our sense of compassion.[7]

How blessed you are if you experience compassion growing within you. The Holy Spirit can help in your quest to be more open, to be more faithful, and to listen more completely.

Jesus, you cared deeply for those you encountered here on earth. Your presence brought peace, hope, and healing. Teach me to be more caring toward others.

The Ginkgo Tree

The ginkgo tree, known to be the oldest tree on earth and revered for its beauty and longevity, is a "living fossil." With its fan-shaped leaves, it has remained unchanged for more than two hundred million years.

My father was very fond of this tree and had one planted near our family grave site. Following an old German custom, my parents would often take my brother, Richard, and me there with a picnic lunch. We would sit under the ginkgo tree and share stories about family.

Years after my father died, I developed a new appreciation for this tree because it reminded me of him. My dad was a very reassuring presence, especially during times of uncertainty.

My husband and I experienced one of those times when an older couple came to live with us for several months. We enjoyed having them, but physically it took a toll on us. We wanted to continue supporting them in our home, but we were torn.

We decided to drive to a favorite place, the Shrine of St. Elizabeth Ann Seton in Emmitsburg, Maryland, to pray about the situation. On the way into the basilica, I looked down at the sidewalk, and there were two perfectly formed fan-shaped leaves side by side. It was as if these gingko leaves had dropped just before we were to reach that spot. But strangely, there was no ginkgo tree to be found in the surrounding area!

We knew my dad, as well as St. Elizabeth Ann Seton, were interceding for us and understood our plight. A deep peace descended on us, and as we looked at one another, we knew that God's grace was sufficient for us (see 2 Corinthians 12:9). We went home to our dear friends with renewed energy and love.

Some might think that our finding the leaves was just a coincidence, but this kind of thing has happened before. It is a reminder that God is with us, as is the company of holy people and saints.

Does my story remind you of a time when you received a sign that reassured you? Or perhaps you were just blessed with an awareness of being loved by God or by a dear one who has gone before you. If so, share your story as an encouragement to someone.

Father, your timing is always perfect. You know when to go before us, and you make it perfectly clear that you have our concerns covered! ⌣

He Touched Me

The New Testament is full of stories about Jesus reaching out to people and healing them and making them whole. And the truth is that Jesus is still reaching out today to heal us—body, mind, soul, and spirit.

Perhaps you have been to a healing Mass, where people come forward and are anointed with oil and prayed over for healing. Perhaps Jesus has healed you in some way through someone's intercession. Jesus also sometimes heals people after they have received the Eucharist.

One day at daily Mass, I had started praying when I realized that my pulse was running very high. I live with the problem of atrial flutter, but it had been some time since my heart rate had been so erratic. I immediately thought, "Should I leave and go to the hospital emergency room, or should I lie down on the pew?" The pressure in my chest got very tight, and my arms felt weightless. I was frightened!

I prayed and asked Jesus for guidance. I began to focus on the Mass, which had just begun. I really wanted to stay. Before I knew it, we were kneeling and praying, "Lord, I am not worthy that you should enter under my roof, but only say the word, and my soul shall be healed." As I went forward, my heart pounding, I focused on the presence of Jesus in the Eucharist. Then, receiving him, I felt my heart peacefully returning to its normal rhythm.

Oh, the joy that flooded my soul! I never expected Jesus' presence in the Eucharist to have such an effect on me. I went through my day, and months afterward, with renewed energy and joy.

Later I told our parish priest what had happened. "I think the most meaningful part of the story is the choice you made to go straight to the Lord—and he took care of you," he said. I often think about that day and am reminded to go to the Lord with whatever it is that is troubling me, ever more confident that he will take care of me.

Each of us can be an example to others as we share our struggles, sufferings, and fears, as well as the difference Jesus makes in our lives.

Jesus, your love has touched my heart time and again, changing my outlook and giving me joy, peace, and renewed love for others. I rejoice in your presence. ⌐

Sharing Stories

As we age, most of us want to have genuine connections with our adult children and grandchildren. Yet building bridges with the next generations can be a challenge because these people have grown up in a much different world than we did. As parents and grandparents, we need to learn how to enter their world through open, loving conversations as well as through telling our stories.

Stories are appealing to all ages but especially to young people. In many cases, we hold the keys to our family history as well as our journey of faith. Telling our stories—ones that highlight virtue, respect, love for others, and working through difficult times—is what turns those keys.

This past Christmas, I was having tea with my daughter, Tina, my two granddaughters, one of my granddaughter's friends, and our grandson Eddie's fiancée. I told a story about Tina showing compassion for her friend Connie many years earlier. Tina, who was ten at the time, had invited Connie over to spend the afternoon. Connie was grieving; her mother had recently died. The two girls were sitting on the hill in our backyard talking, and as I looked out at them, I noticed a flock of white gulls flying down and sitting among them. I was quite surprised at the sight. Then I noticed Connie breaking down and sobbing and Tina moving close to comfort her.

That night Tina told me what had happened. Connie was still struggling with her mother's death and told Tina that God did not exist; if he did, her mother would not have died. Tina tried to reassure her that God does exist and that he loved her. Connie responded, "Well, then ask God to bring those birds down here to sit with us." Tina, with childlike faith, prayed, and a loving Father responded—the birds immediately joined them on the hill!

As we continued to sip tea, each person shared a personal story of hope. There we were, three generations, having a wonderful time telling our stories and building one another up in faith, hope, and love.

I encourage you to think about your life and gather your experiences of God's mercy and love. Ask him to show you how and when you can share these stories, reaching out to others as Jesus has reached out to you.

Father, your love continues to grow from one generation to another. Help me embrace your gift of faith as I share my stories with others. —

A Bad Day

Ever have a bad day, when nothing seems to go right? Perhaps your plans are disrupted, or you are tired and are finding someone particularly irritating. We all have those days. And sometimes "bad days" become a string of "bad weeks" or "bad years."

Whether for a day or a season, trials can hit us hard, especially as we age. Many of us will face changes in our health that will affect our days. Our strength might be limited, as well as our ability to support others. We may be confined to our home and find our need to depend on others frustrating. It may take time for us to come to a place of accepting our circumstances, whatever they may be.

In his book *The Way of Trust and Love*, the renowned author Fr. Jacques Philippe says this:

> What enables us to overcome a trial is not a magic wand that solves everything, but the discovery of what call it is that's being addressed to us, how we're being asked to grow. In understanding and responding to that call, we find new strength, enabling us to get through the trial and make something positive of it. Every trial can

become a path of life, for Christ has risen from the dead and is present everywhere, sowing the seeds of new life in every situation. Even in those that seem most negative and most desperate, God is present.[8]

It's tempting, when faced with difficulties, to question why God is allowing them to happen. We may feel like St. Teresa of Avila. While riding in a carriage on the way to visit one of her convents on a stormy night, she was knocked from the carriage into the mud. Getting up, she said, "Lord, if this is the way you treat your friends, it's no wonder you have so few of them." How refreshing to hear someone use humor when going through a tough time!

Let us take heart, dear friends. Whenever we are going through a bad day or are faced with trials, we can choose to see opportunities to grow in our faith and trust of the Lord. God's transforming love is at work within us!

Father, help me understand your love more fully as I go through trials in my life. ⎯⎯

Decisions about the Future

Making sound decisions about where to live as we age can be difficult, and many of us put off the process of seriously considering the options. This can be problematic. If possible, it's best to make our own decisions or at least join in the process.

Mary was still living alone in an apartment at the age of ninety when her doctor advised her to consider another living situation because of failing health. Her daughter, Pat, and Pat's husband, Bob, who lived in another state, invited her to live with them. Mary decided that she would come for a trial run. Mary stayed nine weeks and had a fine visit but decided it was not for her and returned home. The doctor had told the family that if she did not make her own decision to stay, it probably would not work out.

Pat and Bob received a surprise phone call from Mary four months later. "Is the offer still open for me to come to live with you? I've changed my mind." So Mary returned to the home, where Pat and Bob had updated the bathroom to be "senior friendly" and had arranged a bedroom and sitting room for her on the first floor.

With the help of her daughter, Mary enjoyed making cards and notes to send to those she knew. In time she went to the senior center two days a week. Even with her cognitive changes, she was open to making new friends.

When Mary was dying, Pat invited some friends to drop by for short visits, to sit silently and pray or chat a bit if Mary was awake. By God's grace, Mary was close to Jesus in life and close to Jesus while dying. She said she was ready to "catch the bus and go home." And he came for her just as he promised.

We can learn from Mary how God's grace helped her to make the adjustments she needed in order to finish her life surrounded by peace and love. In the process, he refreshed his gift of love within her, and others were blessed because of her presence. I pray that you and I will take heart by her example as we look ahead to our own future.

Father, you are a loving and caring God. Help me to be willing to ask others for the help I need as I age. ⁓

One Last Gift

When we know a person is dying, we can anticipate something profound going on with him or her. Our God, who is loving and faithful, promises to never leave us or forsake us (see Hebrews 13:5).

When a loved one is dying, we may want to keep a pen and notebook handy, to record what the person says and does in his or her final days. The person may have something special to say that defines a relationship with the living God or with a family member or friend. We can learn a great deal from the person dying, perhaps something we may want to do or say when our time comes.

For the father of a friend of mine, dying was just part of life. He wanted to be surrounded by his children, grandchildren, and great-grandchildren. As Clem was getting close to death, he would say over and over, "I love you, Jesus! Make me more like you." On one occasion, he went on to say, "Oh, I never realized how vast God's mercies are; they seem to have no end. The green pastures—they are enormous; I can't describe their beauty!" These are treasured words that will not be forgotten.

It is also important to let those who are dying know how much we appreciate them and what they have done to inspire us or help us. Two business partners came to visit Clem shortly before he died. They said, "All these years, you have been teaching and training us. First, it was about real estate; next, you taught us so much about life, what is really important. Now you are teaching us how to die."

If needed, we should ask forgiveness of the dying person for anything hurtful we may have said or done over the years. If there is an estranged relationship, we might be able to help arrange a reconciliation.

Even if the dying person is asleep or is in a coma, we can talk directly into their ear, and their soul will absorb our love and our words. Imagine giving a loved one a last gift: your presence and reassurance for the last time, as the person gets ready to travel to our true homeland in heaven.

Father, I don't know when I will pass from this life to the next. Help me to live each day to the fullest, and enable me to be present to others when their times come.

Going beyond Limitations

God calls all of us to be saints, to embrace his deep love for us in such a way that it transforms us day by day into true lovers of God and his people. Because of his love for us, he invites us to have a personal relationship with him. When we pray and allow God to fulfill that desire, we can find an intimacy in his presence that we have never before experienced. What a difference that personal ongoing relationship with the Lord will make in our lives!

Especially as we age, we are confronted with situations in which God seems to be asking us to do things beyond our power. Either we don't have the resources within us, or we don't think we can stretch any further at that particular time. But the power of love from our ongoing relationship with the living God can surprise us, giving us the grace and gifts we need to step out in faith and accomplish what seems to be beyond our capabilities. He can even give us the grace to do this joyfully!

Laura shares her story about her experience with the living God. "It seems there are times when to be able to love requires all that we have. However, God loved me so well during the time I was caring for my mom while she was dying that I, in turn, was able to be creative in blessing her.

"I remember the time when we fixed up a room in our home for her to stay in. I had brought her favorite picture of Jesus and placed it on the bedside table. When she walked in and saw it, she burst out crying.

"For forty-eight years, I felt we had trouble showing love for one another. But in the last eight months of her life, the Lord showed me how I could love my mom in ways that she could accept."

The love God showers on us when we allow ourselves to be loved by him can help us go beyond ourselves and truly accomplish what seems impossible. That's because we are relying not on ourselves but on our Lord, Savior, and Friend!

Father, I don't know what the future holds, but I do know you promise to be with me. Keep me close to you each and every day. ⸺

New Life in Christ

Many people today are giving thought to whom they want to have with them when they are close to death. God our Father is intimately involved with such details of life and death. What a consolation this can be to the dying! God delights in giving them his love and tender care through those close to them.

Anne had a deep love and devotion for Jesus in the Eucharist. Her story is a powerful reminder of what Jesus really meant when he said, "I am with you always" (Matthew 28:20). Her daughter, Marjorie, who is now ninety-four, tells it.

"Momma had been housebound for months prior to her death. The weather was bitter cold, with ice and deep snow on the ground. It had been several weeks since anyone had been able to bring Momma Communion. I suggested we call the rectory and ask once again if someone could come to the house.

"The next day, despite the dangerous weather, a nun arrived at the front door. After spending some time with us and praying with us, she prepared to give Momma Communion. As she raised the host for her, Momma said, 'Oh Jesus, I have been waiting for you!' Anne received Communion and was fully at peace. She died within the hour." Having embraced Jesus in the Eucharist, Anne was ready to go home.

The nun later told the family, "Anne saved my vocation! I was discouraged and ready to resign from my order. This experience changed my life." The nun stayed close to the family. She died just a few years ago.

Pope St. John Paul II said,

I find great peace in thinking of the time when the Lord will call me: from life to life! And so I often find myself saying, with no trace of melancholy, a prayer recited by priests after the celebration of the Eucharist: . . . *At the hour of my death, call me and bid me come to you.* This is the prayer of Christian hope, which in no way detracts from the joy of the present, while entrusting the future to God's gracious and loving care.[9]

Jesus, help me to continue to find joy in your presence, as I, too, entrust the future to your gracious and loving care. ⸺

True to the End

Have you ever known a centenarian? We sometimes read about a person who is celebrating a hundredth birthday. While few of us know someone that age, that could be changing. The number of centenarians is up 44 percent since 2000. Now there are more than seventy-five thousand people in the United States who are over one hundred years of age.

We might wonder, "What if God allows me to live that long? What would my life be like?" Here is a story of two generations of centenarians.

When she was sixty-five years old, Mary Louise and her husband, Clifford, invited her mother to live with them. They helped care for her for five years before she moved into a nursing home close by. Mary Louise went daily to help bathe and feed her mother. She cared for her until she died at age 109. It was a true service of love.

When they were in their nineties, Mary Louise and Clifford decided to move into assisted living. It was there that Mary Louise was widowed. By then her eyesight had grown quite dim, so she got a reading machine to sort out family pictures as well as to read the Bible. She suffered from painful arthritis, making it hard to walk.

God continued to give Mary Louise the gifts of love and perseverance. She was part of a Bible study, and she invited friends to join her for church services. One of her friends had not been to church in fifty years, while another had not been for a very long time. Because of Mary Louise and her encouragement, the two women began attending church with her each week.

At age 103, Mary Louise was still being a light to the people God brought into her life. She was still devoted to God's plan of working through his faithful ones to be his presence in the lives of others. Later that year, Mary Louise was welcomed into the arms of Jesus. She never stopped sharing her faith and doing small things with great love.

Sometimes the smallest act of encouragement can reap great blessings for the ones we reach out to. Who might you reach out to today? How can you love and encourage that person?

Jesus, in your light I do see light (see Psalm 36:9). I desire that you live through me more and more. ⎯

Enjoy a Good Laugh!

We all enjoy being with people who can rise above serious times and find some humor in life. Pope Francis has said how much he likes to laugh. "It helps me feel closer to God and closer to other people. When we laugh with each other and not at each other, God's love is present in a special way."[10]

When was the last time you had a good laugh? If you can't remember, maybe it's been too long. If you think that you really don't have a sense of humor, it may just be underdeveloped. Or perhaps you had one, and now it seems as if you have lost it.

But don't fret—there is hope. According to the Mayo Clinic, a sense of humor can be learned, and more easily than you may think.[11] An article on its website suggests finding photos, greeting cards, and comic strips that make you chuckle and pinning them up at home or in your office. Joke books, old movies, and TV comedy series—all can make us laugh. You may have another idea, uniquely your own. If you do, share it!

One of our favorite sources of humor is the old *I Love Lucy* series. We watched a few of these with our neighbors who are longtime friends, and we couldn't stop laughing. That experience led to a deeper desire to spend some extra time together on a regular basis. From time to time we would share pizza and lots of laughs on Friday nights.

There are many benefits to laughter, according to the report from the Mayo Clinic. Laughter enhances your intake of oxygen-rich air; stimulates your heart, lungs, and muscles; and increases the release of endorphins by your brain. Laughter can have long-term effects, such as improving your immune system and relieving pain. Laughter can also make it easier to cope with difficult situations, and it helps you connect with people.

If you enjoy laughing and often see the humor in situations, consider it a gift that God uses to refresh you and others, and use it often. If you don't have much of a sense of humor, remember, it can be learned. You won't have to look far to find someone who will enjoy a good laugh!

Father, there is a lot of sadness in the world. Help me to laugh with those who laugh and rejoice with my friends and neighbors who rejoice, even when I don't feel like it. ⸺

Worry-Wart

Are you a worry-wart? The term was coined by a cartoonist, J. R. Williams, in 1956. His popular comic strip, *Out Our Way*, featured a character by that name. Worry Wart caused others to worry!

If you're a worry-wart, you're not alone; millions of people have the tendency to worry or be anxious. The good news is that because Jesus came to us in the flesh, he understands our struggles. He even talked about our need to trust in our Father, saying, "Can any of you by worrying add a single hour to your span of life?" (Matthew 6:27).

The best remedy for worry is to bring our concerns about today and the future into our relationship with Jesus. The reality is that we can trust in him and surrender our worries to him. Perhaps as we turn to him in prayer, we can meditate on Scripture passages about worry and anxiety, such as Matthew 6:26-34, Philippians 4:6-7, and Luke 12:22-34.

We also need to remember that God's gifts are available to us as we work against the tendency to worry. After all, he wants us to experience his peace and joy. Asking for his guidance, we can still our thoughts, focusing on his love for us and waiting for him to speak to our hearts. It may be helpful to keep a small journal of what we experience. As we come to him day after day, relying on the Holy Spirit to guide us, we can detect whether a harmful pattern of thought is taking us down that spiral of worry.

Even outside of prayer, as we go about our day, we can gently change the focus of our thoughts of worry to something else. Or we can set aside a certain time of day to give ourselves permission to worry, and we can train ourselves to worry only at that time. We can learn to practice mindfulness, focusing only on the present.

We can even bring in humor about our worry habits. This can put things in perspective. "What do the rocking chair and worry have in common? They both go back and forth and get nowhere!"

Jesus, I know you long for me to find deeper meaning in my life at this time. Help me to trust in you more as I respond to your love, making choices and moving forward. ⸺

Intercessory Prayer Works!

We are truly blessed if we have adopted the habit of interceding for others in prayer. So many wonderful things can come because of our prayers for others. And as we spend time in prayer, interceding for someone or something to change, we may find that we change as well.

Janet prayed for years for her prodigal son. One day she felt the Lord ask her to stop judging her son and to pray for a deeper love and acceptance of him. She did, and in time, she found that she had more peace. She also realized that she needed to make some changes in the way she related to her son. He eventually returned to the family and found peace with God.

Sometimes we are asked to join others in praying for intentions that seem well beyond our reach. Even then we can pray with confidence that divine intervention will prevail.

In July 1863, the Sisters of Charity in Emmitsburg, Maryland, were going about their daily routines. Suddenly they heard horses approaching, and before long, ten thousand Union soldiers were camping on the grounds of their home and school. General Regis de Trobriand looked at the priest who had accompanied him to the observation tower and said, "Get the sisters to pray; there is no guarantee that the coming battle won't be fought on this property."

The sisters decided to ask Our Lady of Victory to intercede with them. For three days they prayed, while feeding the soldiers what food they had. There was much commotion, yet they prayed without ceasing.

On the fourth morning, the soldiers received orders to move to Gettysburg, where the bloodiest battle of the Civil War was eventually fought. In honor of Our Lady of Victory, the sisters had a statue of her placed on their property. That statue is still there today.

Intercessory prayer can change the course of history! If you are not accustomed to this form of prayer, you should seriously consider making it a part of your spiritual life. If you are homebound or limited in your activity, the Church needs you to join her in calling many back to Christ through intercessory prayer. God needs all of us to intercede for his people and his world.

Father, thank you for inviting me to ask great things from you. I trust in your heart of love and mercy. ⸺

Why Attend a Spiritual Retreat?

A recent study of human happiness concluded that our relationships with other people are the most important factor in our personal happiness. What relationship could be more important than our relationship with God? After all, we were created for relationship—with our Father and with others. Created in the image and likeness of God, we have a natural need to form a friendship with our Father through Jesus Christ.

We know that it takes time for a friendship to grow and be strengthened by conversation. During the fifty-three years of our marriage, Frank and I have realized how important communication is in our friendship with one another. Our needs and concerns are ever changing, as are the joys and sorrows we experience. Without good, ongoing communication, we would likely grow further apart.

It is the same with God. That is why the Church encourages us to attend annual retreats, days of reflection, and parish missions. When we get away from our daily routines and concerns at home, we can focus on what our Father wants to say to us, the gifts he wants to give us, and the transformation he is working within us.

God our Father wants your attention! He longs to speak more personally to your heart. He wants to tell you how he delights in you and how he longs for you to more fully understand his love for you. He longs for you to become one with him—one in purpose, mind, and heart. He has indeed gone before you, to prepare a place for you, and someday he will come and take you with him. Don't be afraid of anything; he is with you each step of the way.

Retreats, with the additional time they provide, are important places where your ongoing conversion in Christ can take place. Sometimes he speaks to you about the importance of prayer, service, and sacrifice. He can speak a word of hope or reveal a pattern of weakness or sin. Sometimes he will highlight a single truth that could stay with you for life. Whatever he reveals to you, resolve to embrace his words and his gifts with great love.

Father, I am deeply grateful that you continue to pursue me. Help me carve out time just for you! ⌒

Passing on the Faith

Grandparents have a responsibility to help teach and train their grandchildren in the faith, to pass along what they have learned and experienced in a lifetime. That might sound like a daunting task! Yet with a little forethought and planning, we can find opportunities to share our faith with the younger generation.

As a child, I attended a weeklong Vacation Bible School every summer, where I learned stories about Jesus and came to know him better. I have wonderful memories of those times, and so I decided one summer at the beach to offer our grandchildren their own Vacation Bible School. From the beginning, the children loved it!

I asked my oldest granddaughter, Kristin, who is very creative, to help me. She offered ideas about acting out Scriptures and thought of crafts the children would enjoy. I kept the lessons short and always connected them to something the children could do to help others. At the end of ten days, we put on a show for the parents that depicted what we had learned about Jesus through the Scriptures.

The summer Vacation Bible School spanned eighteen years as more grandchildren were born. Colin, Mae,

Joe, and Mary Claire liked it so much that they asked me to continue it when I came for visits at Thanksgiving and Christmas!

What opportunities might you take advantage of to share your faith with younger members of your family? Perhaps you could take a child to a daily Mass and then out to breakfast. Or you could pray a family Rosary with the grandchildren and talk about the various mysteries. Maybe you could visit a local pilgrimage spot. The possibilities are endless!

Pope Francis has said, "Take home this word of Jesus, carry it in your hearts, share it with the family. It invites us to come to Jesus so that he may give this joy to us and to everyone."[12]

As we pass along our faith, as well as our gifts and talents, God brings deeper meaning into our lives and enriches our families.

Jesus, I know you love my family, for you have shown me many examples of your love over time. Help me realize what more I can share with them and how to make this happen. —

Seeing More Clearly

As I've aged, one of the changes I have noticed is that I have trouble threading a needle, even with my glasses on. But I have found that if I put the needle under a magnifying glass, I can thread it quite easily, and my mending is underway!

The Holy Spirit is just like that magnifying glass. He helps us to see clearly how much God loves us. He enlightens us so that we can understand Scripture. He shows us ways we can love others as God has loved us.

No doubt you can remember someone who has magnified the meaning of God's love or has taught you some other important lesson or skill. It is a fun and meaningful exercise to remember those who have taught us important things.

My mother and grandmother taught me many things; one was the value of sewing and mending. They spent many hours together, sewing and chatting, and they passed along the value of time together as they worked. Their relationship had its challenges, but they worked them out as they did their sewing projects. I learned a lot from them: that it takes time for friendships to grow, that working with our hands to enhance our homes has value, and that mending and sewing for others are expressions of love.

One of the things I enjoy doing is asking our daughter, Tina, if she has any mending for me to do while we are visiting. She usually has some items ready for me to tackle, and it delights my heart! I find time to sit and stitch during a family discussion or when we are watching TV. As I mend, I remember those who have gone before me and who magnified God's love for me, and my heart is flooded with gratitude. Now you know why threading that needle was so important to me!

Who in your past taught you something important? Maybe you can gather a few friends together and share some of your memories with one another. As we recall the lessons we have learned about life, we can thank and pray for those who have passed down their gifts and their wisdom.

Father, thank you for the people in my life who have taught me so many valuable things. How can I be more purposeful in sharing your love and gifts with others? ⌐

Inspired by Love

Statistics speak to the fact that most of us will be in a different living situation in our eighties or nineties. When the time comes to make a change, it will help to see this as a season when God wants to reveal even more of his heart to us. If we approach this time in prayer, he can help us to embrace changes and eventually experience gratitude and even joy in the midst of suffering.

Bob and Marge had never intended to leave Florida, but the doctors gave Bob only two months to live. Their son, Rick, and his wife, Diane, did not want them to be alone, so they invited Bob and Marge to come live with them. Bob and Marge came reluctantly; they did not want to be a burden. Rick and Diane and their family assured them of their love and the gift they would be to them.

There were difficult times as Bob's health declined and he was bedridden. Daily the family prayed, asking for more love to serve. Making changes in schedules, hiring a part-time nurse, at times accepting help from others—in these ways Bob's needs were always met. He lived for another five years, celebrating anniversaries, birthdays, marriages, and babies born within the extended family.

God's love can be magnified even in the midst of suffering with Christ. Marge found growing opportunities to pray and serve her husband in small ways that seemed to please them both. She was by his side daily, helping him with his food, praying the Rosary for special intentions, and finding humor in small things. Friends often stopped by to visit, sometimes to just sit and pray. The great-grandchildren loved to get on the bed with Bob for a few minutes, bringing with them the gift of joy. The priests from the parish brought the Eucharist, along with their own care and concern.

With Christ guiding them, Bob and Marge showed others how to accept changes that come with old age and still find meaning in life. Bob died peacefully at home, with Marge sitting beside him.

Five years later, Marge is still living with her son and his wife. She is an example of the words of Pope Francis: "Happy is the family who have grandparents close by."[13]

Father, you promise to be with me always. Help me to accept and adjust to changes that will come as I age. I trust in your loving embrace. —

Living Hope

I have always understood hope to be an active virtue. It expands as we share it with others. Living with our hope rooted in God is a way of life, the way we naturally think about things.

How can we have more hope in our lives, and how can we share it with others?

In fact, if our hope is not rooted in God, then we can easily be disheartened. Sometimes we need a change of heart. We need to believe that God is always working with us and for us. He wants the best for us and for those whom we love. We cannot give or affirm hope in another if we ourselves are not people of hope.

The younger generation is especially in need of hope. Pope Francis has said, "Our time has a great need for hope! The young can no longer be robbed of hope. . . . The young need hope."[14]

How can we share hope with the younger generation? We can begin by taking the initiative, expressing an interest in their lives, hearing their stories, and telling them ours. We can also follow up on things we've heard from them earlier.

What a wonderful day it is when we can hear the younger generation speak of hope! Recently we asked our grandson Eddie about the pre-Cana conference he had attended with his fiancée, Chelsea. His response gave us much hope for their marriage and life together and for young people in general:

"We learned so much through these talks. They talked about how to work through differences and the importance of listening well and showing respect. They also talked about affirming love, welcoming children, and the value of the sacraments throughout a lifetime."

We can be a people who put our hope in God and trust in his faithfulness and loving presence among us, even as we work through obstacles and sorrows. And then we can share that hope with others, especially the young.

Father, I want to be a person of hope. Help me to believe that you are always for me and not against me, and help me to share hope with others. —

Notes

1. Pope St. John Paul II, Letter to the Elderly, 2, October 1, 1999, http://w2.vatican.va/content/john-paul-ii/en/letters/1999/documents/hf_jp-ii_let_01101999_elderly.html.

2. St. Irenaeus, *Adversus Haeres* 4, 20, 7, quoted in *Catechism of the Catholic Church* (Washington, DC: United States Catholic Conference, 1997), no. 294.

3. St. Cyprian, *Fathers of the Third Century,* vol. 5, ed. Philip Schaff, *Ante-Nicene Fathers,* 465.

4. Pope Francis, Homily, Easter Vigil, March 30, 2013, http://w2.vatican.va/content/francesco/en/homilies/2013/documents/papa-francesco_20130330_veglia-pasquale.html.

5. Pope Francis, Homily at the Celebration of First Vespers of Divine Mercy Sunday, April 11, 2015, http://w2.vatican.va/content/francesco/en/homilies/2015/documents/papa-francesco_20150411_omelia-vespri-divina-misericordia.html.

6. Pope Francis, Address at a Meeting with the Elderly, September 28, 2014, http://w2.vatican.va/content/francesco/en/speeches/2014/september/documents/papa-francesco_20140928_incontro-anziani.html.

7. Robert J. Wicks, *After 50: Spiritually Embracing Your Own Wisdom Years* (Mahwah, NJ: Paulist Press, 1997), 40–41.

8. Jacques Philippe, *The Way of Trust and Love: A Retreat Guide by St. Thérèse of Lisieux* (New York: Scepter, 2012), 125–26.

9. Pope John Paul II, Letter to the Elderly, 17.

10. Pope Francis, note to Fr. Andrew Small, quoted at CBSDC, "Pope Francis Sends Letter to Joke Website: I Like to Laugh a Lot," washington.cbslocal.com/2015/09/24/pope-francis-sends-letter-to-joke-website-i-like-to-laugh-a-lot/.

11. Mayo Clinic Staff, "Stress relief from laughter? It's no joke," mayoclinic.org/healthy-lifestyle/stress-management/in-depth/stress-relief/art-20044456.

12. Pope Francis, Address to Participants in the Pilgrimage of Families during the Year of Faith, October 26, 2013, http://w2.vatican.va/content/francesco/en/speeches/2013/october/documents/papa-francesco_20131026_pellegrinaggio-famiglie.html.

13. Pope Francis, Address at a Meeting with the Elderly.

14. Pope Francis, Audience with Italian Diocese of Cassano all'Jonio in the Region of Calabria, February 21, 2015, as quoted in "Pope's Quotes: A Need for Hope," *National Catholic Reporter,* August 17, 2015, ncronline.org/blogs/francis-chronicles/pope-s-quotes-need-hope.